COMMUNITY AND A

Maintaining quality of life care settings

Simon Evan

ɔhr

This edition published in Great Britain in 2009 by

The Policy Press
University of Bristol
Fourth Floor
Beacon House
Queen's Road
Bristol BS8 1QU
UK

Tel +44 (0)117 331 4054
Fax +44 (0)117 331 4093
e-mail tpp-info@bristol.ac.uk
www.policypress.co.uk

North American office:
The Policy Press
c/o International Specialized Books Services (ISBS)
920 NE 58th Avenue, Suite 300
Portland, OR 97213-3786, USA
Tel +1 503 287 3093
Fax +1 503 280 8832
e-mail info@isbs.com

British Library Cataloguing in Publication Data
A catalogue record for this book is available from the British Library.

Library of Congress Cataloging-in-Publication Data
A catalog record for this book has been requested.

ISBN 978 1 84742 070 1 paperback
ISBN 978 1 84742 071 8 hardcover

Cover design by The Policy Press
Front cover: image kindly supplied by www.istock.com
Printed and bound in Great Britain by TJ International, Padstow

Contents

List of tables, boxes and photos   iv
Acknowledgements   v
Foreword by Judith Phillips   vi

one   Introduction   1

two   What is community?   7

three   Community and ageing   21

four   Housing with care communities in the UK   31

five   An international perspective on retirement villages   59

six   Promoting a sense of community in housing with care settings   71

seven   Diversity, community and social interaction   93

eight   Changing communities and older people   109

nine   Conclusion   125

Appendix   135
References   141
Index   155

List of tables, boxes and photos

Tables

4.1   Models of housing with care and residential care   34
5.1   Ten categories of US retirement villages   61
6.1   Percentage of age group reporting problems accessing a range   81
        of amenities in England (2004–05)

Boxes

4.1   Criteria for a financially viable retirement village location   55
7.1   Accommodation options in retirement villages   95
8.1   Help the Aged's manifesto for lifetime neighbourhoods   113
8.2   Categories of assistive technology, according to function   114

Photos

1   Callendar Court in Gateshead: a council block remodelled as   45
        extra care housing
2   Residents at Monica Wills House in Bristol play snooker in a   77
        communal space (Photograph by Zed Photography)
3   Roof gardening at Monica Wills House in Bristol   80
        (Photograph by Tamany Baker)
4   Painswick retirement village square   85
5   Barton Mews Community Hospital and extra care housing   119

Acknowledgements

I would like thank the many people who have in different ways helped me to write this book.

To my family: Linda, Emily, Ollie and Max, for their love and support and for putting up with my regular mental absences. And to Dexter the dog for providing the excuse for much needed outdoor breaks.

To the colleagues who I worked with on the research projects that have informed this book, including Robin Means, Sarah Vallelly, Tina Fear, Rhonda Knight and James Nicol.

To the many older people and professionals who gave up their time to take part in the research, and the organisations that funded it, including the Joseph Rowntree Foundation, Housing 21, the Housing Corporation and the St Monica Trust.

To Ali Shaw, Emily Watt and everyone else at The Policy Press, whose friendliness and efficiency have made the writing and publication process as painless as possible. They have been a delight to work with.

To those who made invaluable comments on draft versions, including Debra Salmon, Robin Means and a number of anonymous reviewers.

And to Judith Phillips, editor of the Ageing and the Lifecourse series, for her encouragement.

Foreword

Judith Phillips

The study of ageing is continuing to increase rapidly across multiple disciplines. Consequently students, academics, professionals and policy makers need texts on the latest research, theory, policy and practice developments in the field. With new areas of interest in mid- and later life opening up, the series bridges the gaps in the literature as well as providing cutting-edge debate on new and traditional areas of ageing within a lifecourse perspective. Taking this approach, the series addresses 'ageing' (rather than gerontology or 'old age') providing coverage of mid- as well as later life; it promotes a critical perspective and focuses on the social rather than the medical aspects of ageing.

'Housing with care' has become an increasingly important aspect of policy and practice in relation to maintaining independence in later life. There are a burgeoning number of models which, for example, promote such environments as 'extra care' or retirement communities of leisure, activity and well-being. Simon Evans brings together a number of themes and issues around such 'housing with care' models. In doing so he interrogates the notion of community and place, of how the experience of community changes as we age, and provides an insight into the older person and provider aspects of such community living.

The book is an original contribution to the literature drawing not only on UK, but also on European and North American examples. It is informative in relation to the theory, policy and practice around 'housing with care' and is a very timely and comprehensive book that will appeal to a wide audience – students of gerontology, geography, urban studies and urban design, housing specialists, developers and policy makers in this area. It is an invaluable read for those who wish to glimpse into what the future may hold for such communities combining 'housing with care'.

ONE

Introduction

1.1 Introduction

Since the last decade of the 20th century there has been a transformation of the UK retirement housing sector. This is due to a range of factors, including the ageing of the population, increased wealth, greater social mobility and the emergence of an increasingly long post-retirement period, often referred to as the 'third age'. It has also been widely observed that people's expectations for later life have changed considerably, leading to aspirations for a more active and leisure-based retirement lifestyle. Many older people have seen their housing environment as an important element in achieving these goals. As a result, two particular forms of housing for later life have become extremely popular: retirement villages and extra care housing.

The popularity of these two forms of 'housing with care' also reflects the government's focus on supporting independence for older people in their own homes, in settings where flexible care packages are also available. In this respect these two forms of provision are widely perceived as providing a domestic environment, in contrast to the more institutionalised setting of care homes. This has led to these settings being described as a 'third way', between living in the community and in residential care. Further reasons for their popularity include the unsuitability of much general housing for older people and a feeling among many retired people that society is increasingly failing to take account of their needs and preferences. This has led to a focus on these two forms of housing with care as 'communities' that have been designed specifically and exclusively for older people. This is reflected in marketing campaigns that portray them as places in which residents can enjoy a worry-free later life, doing the things they enjoy with 'like-minded' people.

In this book I explore the characteristics of extra care housing and retirement villages, and chart their development in the UK, the US and around the world. I also discuss their role in promoting quality of life for older people and the extent to which they are experienced as communities by those who live in them. These issues are explored in the context of theories of community and ageing, particularly in relation to the built environment and social interaction.

1.2 Housing in an ageing society

The demographics of our ageing society are by now familiar to most of us. For example, 17 million people in the UK are aged over 55, 2,800 people are turning 60 every day and there will be three million people over the age of 65 by 2020. Similarly, in the US there will be 22 million Americans aged over 65 by 2030 and one million over the age of 100 by 2040. These trends will continue for several decades as life expectancies continue to increase and the 'baby boomer' generation – the large number of people born after the Second World War and during the 1960s – grow older. Of particular interest to this book are the implications of these trends for housing and care. As growing numbers of older people come to the end of full-time employment and look forward to many years of retirement, sometimes called the 'third age', they are increasingly seeing the quality and location of their housing as central to their quality of life and to their aspirations.

The majority of people express a strong desire to remain living independently in their own homes as they grow older and most will remain in general housing, but increasing numbers are looking to specialist forms of housing with care as an option that can fulfil their lifestyle choices while at the same time offering the levels of care and support that they need now or might need in the future. This demand is partly driven by the fact that much general housing is not suitable for older people who need care. In England, 33% of homes occupied by older people fail the decent homes standard, which equates to approximately 1.8 million households. At the same time there is a lack of appropriate services for older people who want to be cared for at home. Between 2000 and 2006 the number of households receiving home care decreased by over 13%. Two forms of housing with care that particularly aim to meet the demand for independence and active ageing lifestyles are retirement villages and extra care housing, also known as assisted living facilities. These two forms of provision share several key characteristics. Both are age restricted (residency is usually open to those aged 55 and over), cater for a range of levels of care needs, have 24-hour care staff and provide a range of onsite facilities and services.

Both of these forms of housing are constantly evolving, which makes it difficult to offer accurate definitions, although this is attempted in Chapter Four. However, it is possible to identify three ways in which extra care housing and retirement villages often differ. First, although both offer housing and a range of care options, a large majority of extra care residents have some form of care package, while many of those living in retirement villages receive no care at all. The second common difference is in terms of scale. Extra care schemes usually range in size, from a few bungalows to over 50 flats, while retirement villages tend to contain over 100 units of housing, with the largest in the UK now approaching about 600 units and some in the US providing housing for over 75,000 residents. Third, extra care housing schemes are often situated in the suburbs of towns and cities, while retirement villages usually have a much more rural location, largely due to the amount of land they require. This has a number of implications in terms of their connections with wider communities and social networks, which will be explored throughout this book. In addition to a philosophy of promoting independence for their residents, both of these forms of provision tap into the aspirations of many older people to belong to a community. This is reflected in marketing campaigns based on slogans such as 'forge new friendships with like-minded people who share your interests, your joys and your challenges in life' and 'peace, security and above all a real sense of community'. There is plenty of evidence to suggest that older people are indeed looking for a sense of community, but what does community mean to older people, how do experiences of community change across the lifecourse, and to what extent can aspirations for community be met in these settings? These questions are at the core of this book. A range of factors are explored, including the role of social networks, the availability of activities and facilities and the impact of the built environment. In addition, the role of diversity in communities is considered in the context of settings that are, by their nature, age segregated.

This book draws on a broad research and literature base from a range of disciplines, including social gerontology, sociology, environmental psychology and community studies. The findings from three projects in particular with which the author was involved are prominently featured. These projects are summarised here and a full description of each is provided in the Appendix.

1) Vallelly, Evans, Fear and Means (2006), Opening doors to independence: a longitudinal study exploring the contribution of extra care housing to the care and support of older people with dementia.

This innovative study used a tracking approach to explore the extent to which extra care housing can support people with dementia as their illness progressed. A longitudinal approach was employed to collect quantitative data from 15 extra care schemes across England. In addition, a series of indepth interviews were carried out with residents with dementia, other residents, scheme staff and other professional stakeholders in five schemes over the same period. A range of factors were found to be particularly important to promoting quality of life for residents with dementia, including good design, flexible care provision, staff training, links to the wider community and a realistic approach to risk. This work is one of few studies to take a longitudinal approach to people with dementia in housing with care settings.

2) Evans and Means (2007), Balanced retirement communities? A case study of Westbury Fields.

Westbury Fields, a gated development in the suburbs of Bristol, was one of the first UK retirement villages to include a range of tenures across a single site, by combining privately owned retirement apartments with extra care housing and a nursing care home. This study used qualitative and quantitative research methods within a case study design to explore levels and types of social interaction across tenures and the extent to which residents felt that they were part of a broad community. The study concluded that several features affected the development of a community in this setting, including the physical layout of the village, the provision and location of facilities together with activities and the extent to which village residents are able to engage with local neighbourhoods.

3) Evans and Vallelly (2007), *Promoting social wellbeing in extra care housing.*

Six extra care schemes across England were selected as case studies for this project, in order to explore best practice for promoting social wellbeing among residents. Six key factors emerged as crucial: friendship and social interaction, the provision of facilities, the built environment, the philosophy of care, engagement with the local community and the role of family carers. A literature review carried out as part of this work highlighted the crucial role of social wellbeing in independence and quality of life for older people in housing with care settings.

1.3 The structure of the book

Chapter Two considers the role of concepts of 'community' in society and explores how theories and definitions have changed over time. 'Community' has always been a key concept in the development of culture and society, and many writers have lamented the passing of an 'idyllic' village past, to be replaced with the discord and divisions of the urban present. Others have suggested that such sentiments are unrealistic and that communities are dynamic entities based on diversity and conflict. A range of theories are explored, including community of interest, community of place, community of identity and community in place. A range of socio-economic factors are examined in this context, including social networks, globalisation and social mobility. The concepts of neighbourhood and community are compared, along with the differences between rural and urban communities. The nature and impact of government policy on community is considered, particularly in terms of the recent emphasis on promoting community as an important element in the quality of life and wellbeing of older people.

Chapter Three focuses on how ideas and experiences of community change as we grow older. Recent cohorts of retirees are less likely to have experienced more traditional communities and tend to have less class solidarity, but what are the implications of this for our community aspirations as we age? Communities have in the past helped to provide stability and continuity but social changes, such as the closure of many local services and facilities, have changed the role of the local area for many people. The meaning of community for older people is also explored in the context of weakening intergenerational links as a result of the increased social, occupational and geographical mobility of young people. In exploring how these changes affect older people in particular, this chapter argues that community continues to be important, and that well-designed, accessible housing is a key component in promoting community involvement and quality of life.

Chapter Four provides an overview of housing with care settings in the UK and examines their increasing popularity in recent years. A range of reasons for this rapid growth are discussed, such as the ageing population, the concept of ageing in place, the development of new lifestyles in older life and a general recognition of the need for greater choice and flexibility in housing options for older people. A history of the development of housing with care schemes is presented, from the communities for retired soldiers in Roman times (Bernard, 2008), through the emergence of extra care schemes in the late 1900s to the recent trend for increasingly large retirement villages. The common characteristics of such schemes are described, including a range of facilities, social activities and flexible care packages. The chapter finishes by examining how housing with care schemes are marketed with images of vibrant communities that offer a positive lifestyle for older people, incorporating successful ageing and the concept of a worry-free active retirement.

Chapter Five is concerned with the development of housing and care options for older people outside the UK. This chapter examines how retirement 'communities' first appeared in Europe as schemes with religious affiliations to shelter and care for the aged and then spread to the US, where about 2,000 of them had been built by 2001. It also describes how they have become established as a popular form of retirement housing in Australia and New Zealand and are now appearing in many other parts of the world.

An exploration of how community is conceptualised, promoted and perceived in housing with care settings is provided in Chapter Six. This includes a consideration of how providers have attempted to create communities in extra care schemes and retirement villages and the extent to which residents experience them as such. The importance of a wide range of factors is considered in promoting and maintaining community in housing with care, including social capital, the provision of facilities, design factors and interaction with the wider community. The roles of community in supporting quality of life and social wellbeing are identified. The challenges to promoting community in housing with care settings are discussed, including age segregation, impaired mobility and reduced cognitive function. Opportunities to interact with the wider community are crucial to many of those living in housing and care settings. This chapter also explores how such opportunities can be promoted, and looks at some of the potential challenges, including access to transport, design factors and location. The nature of gated communities is also considered in this respect.

Modern housing with care schemes are marketed as communities that support active ageing for a population that is increasingly diverse in terms of age, cognitive functioning, mobility, health status, care needs, lifestyles and aspirations. Chapter Seven explores the extent to which such diversity is supported in housing with care settings and examines the potential for social exclusion and isolation. Mixed tenure is explored as a strategy for encouraging diversity, as are features such as 'pepperpotting' and 'tenure blind' that have been used in these settings. A number of challenges to supporting diversity are identified, including a lack of clear information about the nature of such communities, tensions between residents from different socio-economic backgrounds and a lack of tolerance of different lifestyles. This chapter will also look at the age-segregated nature of most housing and care environments and the implications of this for the concept of community. A range of other factors are identified as important to diversity, including the siting of community facilities, the availability of inclusive activities and accessible design.

Chaper Eight considers how communities might continue to change over the next 20 years and the impact these changes might have on the quality of life of older people. This includes a look at the main factors that are likely to affect the role of community, including the delivery of services, increasing use of technology and telecare, the transport infrastructure, the supply and design of housing, older people's needs and aspirations and other social changes. For example, while internet shopping is beginning to affect the provision of local essential services, only 20% of older people use computers and the internet. The chapter suggests that many older people wish to remain economically active and to enjoy increased levels of participation in voluntary and social enterprise activities. It is argued that it is therefore vital to take into account the aspirations of older people and to facilitate their desire to contribute towards the communities in which they live, rather than seeing them as a burden on those communities. The future of retirement villages and extra care housing is considered in the context of social changes, particularly in terms of their ability to work as communities.

Chapter Nine provides a review of theories of community in relation to housing with care settings. I argue that, despite a range of social changes, physical place remains important as a venue for social interaction, particularly for older people who tend to spend more time in their local neighbourhood than do other age groups. The continued popularity of extra care housing and retirement villages is examined in the context of older people's aspirations, their experiences of living in societies that are increasingly age focused and their power as consumers. Finally, I explore the key question of whether these settings can really function as sustainable communities.

TWO

What is community?

2.1 Introduction

The concept of 'community' has always featured strongly in the development of culture and society. Many writers have lamented the passing of the 'idyllic' rural-style community and its replacement with the discord and divisions that are perceived to be prevalent in present-day urban living. This chapter explores definitions and theories of community and how they have changed. For example, while early commentators focused on the role of place in a sense of community, some theorists now see communities of interest as more predominant and suggest that kinship has become less important than broader social networks. At the same time, strong communities based on religious identity are emerging, and globalisation has led to social identities becoming blurred and less rooted in physical places.

The impact of government policy on community is also considered, particularly in light of the recent emphasis on promoting community engagement for older people as an important element in quality of life and wellbeing. For example, in the last four years the government has required local authorities to develop community strategies, published a White Paper entitled 'Strong and Prosperous Communities' (Department for Communities and Local Government (DCLG), 2006), launched its Sustainable Communities plan and created the post of minister for community cohesion. Community, it would seem, is firmly back at the top of the agenda.

2.2 What is 'community'?

Unless you are a hermit you probably feel part of at least one community and quite possibly several. In fact, even some hermits used to live in communities. In the 12th century hermits calling themselves the Brothers of the Blessed Virgin Mary were to be found in groups on Mount Carmel, living a life of prayer together. The concept of community is a strong thread running through our society, falling in and out of fashion but ever present. It has enjoyed a resurgence of late, as demonstrated by its appearance at the centre of a raft of public policies and initiatives, such as 'care in the community', numerous community development initiatives and the Sustainable Communities agenda. This reflects widespread concern at the weakened status of community in modern society and a fear that it is being replaced by individualism, consumerism and greed. The observation that society has suffered from a loss of community is also a recurrent theme in the literature, from Durkheim's concept of 'anomie' (1951) – a social state in which mutual bonds and obligations disappear in the face of unchecked individualism – to a recent survey that found that the decline of community was seen as one of the greatest 'social evils' (Watts, 2008). As Taylor (2008) pointed out, the 'lost community mantra' has been recited at frequent intervals over the centuries.

For a concept that is still so widely used, 'community' is extremely difficult to pin down and it has been suggested that it means something different to everyone (Crow and Allan, 1994). The *Oxford English Dictionary* defines community as 'a group of people living together in one place' and 'the people of an area or country considered collectively'. Such groups are connected by 'a common religion, race, or profession' and 'the holding of certain attitudes and interests in common'. Similarly, the *Cambridge Dictionary of American English* defines a community as 'all the people who live in a particular area, or a group of people who are considered as a unit because of their shared interests, background, or nationality'. These definitions might be viewed as simplistic, but they do reflect the three elements that are commonly found in theories of community: place, interest and identity.

2.3 Theories of community

Identification with physical place has traditionally been seen as the most significant element of a sense of community. This is based on the assumption that people develop a sense of identity with others who live in the same geographical area. These theories, which are often known as theories of 'community of place', also acknowledge a role, albeit a lesser one, for shared interests in creating a sense of community. Tönnies and Loomis (1957) were some of the first sociologists to explore concepts of community. They coined the term '*gemeinschaft*' to indicate social relations that are close-knit and intimate because they take place in a well-defined physical space, such as a rural village. They contrasted this to '*gesellschaft*', a looser type of relationship based on associations that were less personal and intense. Both Tönnies and Loomis (1957) and Durkheim (1964) saw community as fundamentally good, a source of social order, and suggested that the breakdown of community was responsible for various social ills. Research case studies from sociology and community development at that time tended to reflect this focus, portraying villages and small towns as harmonious, idyllic communities. In 1969 an article by an eminent sociologist (Stacey, 1969), 'The myth of community studies', did much to discourage the concept of community. Stacey found such theories rather lifeless and preferred to talk about local social networks instead. Part of the attraction of this approach is that social networks can be explored and diagramatically mapped in terms of connectedness. This model of 'network mapping' was further developed by Antonucci et al (1998), who placed network members in three concentric circles according to feelings of closeness. Using this method, Fiori et al (2008) identified four network types: diverse, restricted, friend-focused and family-focused. Other theories of social networks, such as the 'theory of functional specificity' (Weiss, 1974) and the 'convoy model of social relations' (Kahn and Antonucci, 1980), emphasised that it is not only the structure of social networks but also their function that is important. This approach suggests that different relationships have different functions for the individual, fulfilling a different purpose in relation to maintaining physical and mental wellbeing. It is suggested that social networks that contain diverse members are better for the individual's health and wellbeing than networks that are more homogenous. Wenger (1995) developed this idea further in her study of older people in Wales and identified several types of support network. These were defined according to three criteria: the availability of close kin; the level of involvement of family, friends and neighbours; and the level of interaction with voluntary and community groups.

Community re-emerged as a popular concept in sociology, with the focus increasingly on factors other than place as the key element. For example, Willmott (1989) suggested that community is about people who share some element of identity or belonging. This might be a specific territory, such as a street, a town, or a country, but he felt that increasingly it was an element that was not related to place, such as ethnic background, a leisure interest, religious belief or political affiliation. Pahl (1970) also challenged traditional theories of community that focus on physical place. For him, all communities were communities of the mind, an illusion that we adopt in order to create a feeling of control and autonomy over our lives. Similarly, Cohen (1985) described communities as a largely personal or symbolic construct that defines our identity and distinguishes between members and non-members. To this extent we each have our own unique perception and experience of community. He also argued that the idea of community is largely a construction of the media, with particular communities becoming labelled as dangerous due, for example, to levels of drug use and crime. It is these perceptions, he suggested, that lead some older people to seek the relative safety of purpose-built settings.

However, despite social change and the development of wider social networks, there is plenty of evidence to suggest that place-based communities are still important. For example, the Institute of Public Policy Research (Nash and Christie, 2003) reported that communities of place are still important to many people, particularly those with family and friends close by. Similarly, a Home Office citizenship survey (Attwood et al, 2002) found that knowing and spending time with people can help build local social networks, develop trust and promote involvement in community activities. More recently a survey of 1,000 adults (Marsh, 2006) concluded that, contrary to popular opinion, community and neighbourhood are not in decline, particularly among older people.

A range of reasons have been proposed for the importance of place in community attachment. Munro (1995) suggested that specific physical features – a physical landmark or a particular building, for example – contribute towards strong identity with place. A recent example can be seen in new urban developments such as the Millennium Village in Greenwich, where the grouping of houses around a green or lake are attempts to create social connections that focus on strong place-based features. Lee and Newby (1983) described three types of community that are similar to place-based, identity-based and interest-based communities. They call them locality (purely physical), local social systems (based on interaction) and communion (a shared sense of identity). Taking these theories further, a close-knit community can be seen as one in which the three dimensions (place, interest and identity) overlap to a greater extent. The widespread focus on three main elements of community has been challenged as simplistic. For example, Calhoun (1980) argued that communities of interest are too one dimensional to count as truly communal settings, while Gilleard and Higgs (2000) hypothesise that communities based on shared interest are less exclusive than those based on identity and suggest that the term 'coalitions of interest' is more appropriate than 'communities of interest'.

Many modern theorists have focused on the impact of globalisation on community, suggesting that mutual solidarities have been replaced by fragmentation and disengagement (for example Phillipson, 1997; Beck, 2000; Bauman, 2001). For Brent (2004), the concept of community is often used in a way that denies the impact of wider forces such as globalisation and capitalism, in an attempt to escape the uncertainties of social reality. He argued that while current usage of the term tends to focus on an idyllic state of social harmony, in reality community is about movement and change. He concluded that the only meaningful definition of community is in relation to the very desire for community itself, which continues to be influential on both an individual and a collective level.

The phenomenal growth in popularity of online communities that flourish in the absence of face-to-face contact is often seen as evidence in support of the argument that the geographical element of community is becoming less important. The key factor here is not shared physical space but contact of a social kind (Anderson, 1991). This shift in focus from geographical place to social interaction as the key feature of community can be seen in the work of Frankenberg. In 1967 he borrowed a definition of community from Maciver and Page (1950) as 'an area of social living marked by some degree of social coherence' (p 271). However, by 1982 his thinking had led him to use the following definition of community: 'A lot of people co-operating and disputing within the limits of an established system of relations and cultures' (p 5).

More recent studies support this focus on social interaction as the key element in a sense of community. For example, a study of three Scottish housing developments (Robertson et al, 2008) concluded that understandings of 'community' were rooted in fleeting, everyday interactions, such as chatting at the post office or hairdressers, which were often enough to give people a powerful sense of attachment and belonging. There is also ample evidence of the role of social relations in maintaining quality of life for older people. A range of specific benefits from higher levels of social interaction have been identified, including improved health and wellbeing (Gilbart and Hirdes, 2000), lower rates of depression (Godfrey et al,

2004), decreased risk of dementia (Sugisawa et al, 2002) and even lower mortality rates (Flacker and Kiely, 2003). Social networks have a dual function: the provision of social support and social connectedness. Three types of social support have been identified by House et al (1985): emotional support, instrumental support and appraisal support. These can all contribute towards self-esteem and a sense of belonging. Social connectedness is created through the pleasurable nature of social interaction, which satisfies the human need for social and emotional contact (Ashida and Heaney, 2008).

Some writers have suggested that concepts of past communities have been romanticised and that the three dimensions of place, interest and identity remain important. They may overlap less than they used to but they never were completely coterminous. Most commentators agree that our concept of community has become diluted and is less dependent on attachment to place than in the past. It may be, as Gilleard and Higgs (2000) suggest, that, while in the past most people had a strong attachment to a single community of place, we are now more likely to feel that we belong to multiple communities that are not connected in any way. For example, some of us may feel part of one community where we live, another where we work and a third in relation to a particular leisure interest. It may also be the case that for many of us our membership of the community of place where we live is automatic and largely arbitrary, merely by dint of living there rather than having any real sense of active involvement or interaction.

At the heart of the difficulties in defining community is the fact that the same word is often used in two different ways: at a physical level focusing on place and at a more conceptual level as a value. Calhoun (1980) recognised this when he wrote about communities of propinquity, which focus on geographical space, and community as a variable in the form of social relations. This dual meaning of community is taken further by Gilleard et al (2007), who describe one form as social space and the other as a collective consciousness of social connection. According to Pahl (1970), to these could be added a third: individual consciousness – real or illusory – of social connection.

The American sociologist Putnam has made a major contribution to contemporary theory of community. He introduced the term 'social capital' to describe networks of social connection. He defined this as 'the features of social life – networks, norms and trust – that enable participants to act together more effectively to pursue shared objectives' (Putnam, 1995: 667). He distinguished between two types of social capital: bonding social capital, which is formed of closed networks of strong ties among family members, close friends and neighbours; and bridging social capital, which takes the form of overlapping networks of weaker ties. To a large extent community and social capital are indistinguishable in the literature, with both implying a range of characteristics of human relations, including trust, cooperation, reciprocity and responsibility. Colclough and Sitaraman (2005) suggest that they are fundamentally different concepts and that social capital networks are much more task driven, containing a strong element of instrumentalism and purpose. They imply that individuals have taken a conscious decision to dedicate resources in the expectation of specific outcomes, hence the term 'capital'. Communities, in contrast, are created by social relationships that derive from common experiences that lead to attachment among members. These writers also identify two types of community: simple communities, which are small, place based and tend to contain one or a few groups that span a single domain of everyday life; and complex communities, which involve a larger number of overlapping groups such as work, family and friends.

Changes in types and patterns of social interaction have led to the development of new uses of the word 'community', in particular online communities. These can be a challenge to traditional concepts of community because they are completely independent of physical place. However, they also share a number of key characteristics, and the internet can be seen to some extent as a virtual place that serves as a venue for social interaction just as a coffee shop might. Online communities are discussed in more detail in Chapter Eight. For many environmental psychologists, place attachment is a key factor in a sense of community. Livingstone (1995) defined place attachment as the emotional or affective bonds that individuals have to particular places, including the neighbourhood in which they live. He suggested that we make stronger bonds with a place if it meets our physical and psychological needs and matches our goals and lifestyle. Similarly, Stokowski (2002) identified two types of attachment to place: functional and emotional. Functional attachment is the ability of a place to enable us to achieve our goals and desired activities, while emotional attachment refers to the feelings, moods and emotions people have about certain places. This is particularly important in terms of developing and maintaining a sense of identity and self-esteem. According to Giuliani and Feldman (1993), place attachment is a kind of psychological investment in a place that develops over time and is encouraged by distinctiveness, continuity and self-esteem.

Other environmental psychologists have developed more specific theories of community. Kasarda and Janowitz (1974) distinguished between a linear model of community, whereby increases in city population and density reduce the significance of community, and a systemic model that sees friendship, kinship and ties as central to the development of community. Their study of data from Great Britain included three elements as measures of community attachment: feelings of belonging, interest in the local area and feelings about leaving. Their findings indicated that length of residence was the most important factor in a sense of belonging to the community and that the number of local friends was most positively associated with stronger community sentiments, followed by the number of local relatives. Similar findings were reported by Woolever (1992) from a study carried out in the city of Indianapolis in Indiana. Here again, higher population density was associated with lower levels of attachment and involvement. The main drivers of place attachment were home ownership, levels of education, age and length of residence. Differences in income and ethnic composition were not significant predictors of attachment to place. A range of factors that mitigate against a sense of attachment were highlighted by Sampson (1988), including urbanisation, fear of crime and the population density of children.

2.4 Community and public policy

Despite the difficulties of definition, community is, as Crow and Allan (1994) maintain, a concept that won't lie down. It certainly has a long history in public policy, particularly since the late 1960s where it became prevalent through recognition of the need for public participation. In this respect community has often been seen as a force for moral good and public order. As a result, public policy has tended to focus on attempts to create community where it is thought to be lacking, for example in under-privileged neighbourhoods where social interaction is dysfunctional. In this respect neighbourhood is seen as the most effective area in which to re-engage individuals and reforge links between people to generate a sense of belonging and identity (Montgomery, 2006). During the 1980s and early 1990s deficits in the physical infrastructure were seen by government as the main reasons for problems in deprived communities. The response of Thatcherism was to support global corporations to operate in these areas, on the basis that the resultant economic benefits would trickle down to those in poverty. Unfortunately this trickle-down effect did not become apparent.

The concept of community has enjoyed a resurgence under New Labour and is at the core of UK government thinking. It has become firmly established at the centre of a wide range of government initiatives, policies and strategies, including care in the community, community policing, community development and sustainable communities, to name but a few. This overall approach is based on the principle that the breakdown of community is the main reason for social problems. The government's policy focus has therefore been on social inclusion and community involvement, as demonstrated by the creation of the Department of Communities and Local Government (DCLG), with its vision of 'prosperous and cohesive communities', offering a safe, healthy and sustainable environment for all (DCLG, 2006: 47).

Recent government policy has also focused on strong neighbourhoods as crucial to promoting social cohesion. For example, the Neighbourhood Renewal Strategy aims to make a major contribution to tackling social exclusion and deprivation (Social Exclusion Unit, 1998). The attraction of neighbourhood as a concept appears to be a practical one, in that it provides a manageable framework within which community development work can be channelled. Meegan and Mitchell (2001) suggest that the key feature distinguishing neighbourhood from community is that the former is essentially a living space through which people pass on a daily basis with the purpose of accessing social and material resources. Community, in comparison, is based on broader networks of social interaction and does not necessarily imply the same level of instrumentalism or purpose. Forrest and Bridge (2006) also highlight the importance of neighbourhood as a source of social identity and informal assistance, although they acknowledge the fact that there are an increasing number of other sources. They define neighbouring as 'the exchange of small services or support in an emergency against a background of routine convivial exchanges' (p 14). They contrast manifest neighbouring, which is face-to-face social interaction, with a more general sense of belonging and responsibility to an area, which they call latent neighbouring. They also note that concepts of 'good' neighbouring can depend on class and culture and that in some situations keeping to oneself can be seen as good neighbouring. For Abrams and Bulmer (1986), neighbourliness can bring a range of benefits, including higher house values, lowered anxiety about crime, a clean and attractive environment and a stronger sense of belonging and social identity. They suggested that neighbourhoods offer a comfortable balance between social connectedness and remoteness.

Similarly, Davies and Herbert (1993) conceptualise neighbourhood rather neatly in terms of the immediate space around a residence, in which people engage in 'neighbouring'. This they define as 'a set of informal face to face interactions based on residential proximity' (Davies and Herbert, 1993: 1). Seabrook (1984) discussed neighbourhood in terms of familiarity, as an area where the majority of people know by sight the majority of people who live there. It can be argued that neighbourhood has heightened importance for certain groups, including older people, and this is something this book will come back to in Chapter Three. Conversely, neighbourhood might be less important to the better-off, who can more easily choose the extent to which their social life revolves around family and neighbours. Thomas (1983) calls these nominal communities, which are characterised by a lack of or infrequency of interactions between residents. While neighbourhood has become a key spatial unit in UK government policy, largely in terms of rebuilding social capital in disadvantaged areas, it is to some extent a matter of terminology rather than substance, and many writers have argued that community remains important for urban regeneration and social inclusion (Henderson, 2003).

This renewed enthusiasm for community on the part of government, as sometimes expressed through neighbourhood initiatives, was largely prompted by concerns about the integration of immigrants and the rioting that took place in several cities in northern England during 2001. As a result, the concept of community is also a major element in the new framework governing race-relations policy in the UK (Worley, 2005). These concerns jolted politicians into supporting a range of initiatives that promote community cohesion. For example, as part of the modernisation of local government, New Labour placed a duty on county and district councils to demonstrate 'effective community leadership' by developing community strategies (2000 Local Government Act). These were based on improving the economic, social and environmental wellbeing of their areas and providing public services that are 'responsive to the needs and concerns of local communities'. This agenda was taken a step further by the 2007 Sustainable Communities Act, which replaced community strategies with 'sustainable' community strategies and invited local authorities to make proposals that could promote the economic, social or environmental wellbeing of their area. Sandwiched between these two initiatives was the White Paper entitled *Strong and Prosperous Communities*, which aimed to give communities more influence and the power to improve their lives, shape neighbourhoods and 'foster a sense of community and civic pride' (DCLG, 2006: 5). This was to be achieved through a rebalancing of the relationship between central government, local government and local people. Specific measures included neighbourhood charters that set out local standards and priorities, encouraging councils to work more closely with neighbourhood policing teams, giving councillors small budgets, providing support for community groups and exploring how communities could manage or own community assets. In addition, county councils became responsible for preparing delivery plans for the sustainable community strategies, known as local area agreements.

Taken together then, these policies emphasise the value placed on community by government as a key force for moral good and social order in a democratic society. Imrie and Raco (2003) provide a list of over 40 policy programmes that focus on community, including Active Community Units, the Community Empowerment Fund and Community Chests. Interestingly, many of these adopt a spatial approach to community. For example, Health Action Zones, Employment Action Zones and New Deal for Communities all identify community in physical terms. 'Community cohesion' has now joined 'sustainable communities' on the list of current political buzzwords, as demonstrated by the formation of a Community Cohesion Unit within the Home Office in 2001.

The restoration of community has been a major policy objective, while at the same time supporting the development of communities that are socially cohesive and sustainable is seen as the best way to tackle a range of social issues, including crime, health and education. Compared with earlier approaches, this is governance by community rather than by market or state, with a firm focus on the role of community as a source of moral good. This has been described as moral, authoritarian communitarianism (Etzioni, 1995) as a result of its emphasis on balancing the rights of the individual with social responsibilities and its focus on the revival of social structures such as parenting, the family and voluntary associations. In exploring the debates about social cohesion in relation to urban governance, Kearns and Forrest defined social cohesion in terms of 'component parts that fit in and contribute to society's collective project and wellbeing' (2000: 996). Despite the range of initiatives that have been put in place (for example the Institute of Community Cohesion, the Commission on Integration and Cohesion; the Housing Corporation Community Cohesion Strategy, to name but a few), they concluded that there is a lack of real evidence to support the social cohesion agenda.

This reflects wider scepticism about the enthusiasm with which New Labour has embraced community as an answer to a range of social problems. Burnett (2007) describes the drive towards communities based on common principles as a 'civilising project', while Levitas (2000) highlights the 'promiscuous flexibility' with which New Labour uses the term 'community' and concludes that it is used to mask both the impact of economic relationships in social conflict and the role of the state in imposing order. Instead, crime is attributed to the breakdown of community, and community values are imposed through schooling, parenting and sanctions. Several reasons have been suggested for this almost obsessive focus of government policy on community. These include an attempt to shift responsibility for social problems onto local communities, a desire to avoid the social divisions that are so evident in some cities in the US, and the desire to be different from the preceding Conservative governments. Whatever the reasons, this policy approach to community appears to be based on the assumption that the ideal community is a socially cohesive unit. It is based on the premise that social exclusion is about disconnection from society, and therefore restoring community will help people to reconnect and rediscover their sense of social responsibility. To a large extent this approach leans on concepts of social capital as developed by Bourdieu (1986), Putnam (1995) and others. It sees lack of social capital as the main reason for the underperformance of some citizens in the social, cultural and economic spheres and therefore the main cause of social exclusion. It therefore aims to increase social inclusion by developing the networks, norms and trust that social capital implies, thus restoring cohesive communities.

However, this whole approach assumes that community is exclusively positive and has no disadvantages, an assumption that has been widely challenged. For example, Atkinson (2003) suggests that communities can be oppressive and conformist, while social capital often acts as an elitist commodity rather than a public good. Similarly, Raco (2003) states that current government policy ignores both the role of communities of interest and the dynamics of difference within any community. He argues that because membership is implicit in the concept of community so is non-membership, which is basically a form of social exclusion. This corresponds with Edwards' (2003) argument that the focus on community and social cohesion masks diversity and makes certain groups, such as disabled people, relatively invisible. A review of the evidence for tackling place-based deprivation concluded that place attachment that is based on strong family and social networks in deprived neighbourhoods can limit people's aspirations and willingness to consider opportunities elsewhere (Taylor, 2008).

It can be argued, therefore, that recent government policy is based on a greatly simplified notion of community. Under this view of community as a tool of social policy, community is something that is imposed from the outside as an attempt to create unity. Many authors suggest that community is by nature based on diversity rather than unity. Brent (1997) characterises community as multidimensional in nature and based on division. This is borne out by the findings of a study on immigration and social cohesion carried out in six UK cities (Hickman et al, 2008). Most people interviewed felt that social cohesion was to do with achieving a balance between difference and unity in local areas, rather than expecting complete consensus on values and priorities.

2.5 Community and housing

Many studies have explored the impact of the built environment on the development of a sense of community. This has been framed largely in terms of the extent to which physical design and layout provide opportunities for social interaction between residents. Robertson et al (2008) found that housing style, spatial layout and the relationship of housing to public open space are key to neighbourhood identity. They also commented on the intrusive nature of car traffic for the development of a sense of community, and suggested that car-free street environments can encourage social interaction. They concluded that the way in which housing developments are planned has a long and sustained impact in terms of fostering social interactions. There is also evidence that older residents of higher-quality homes feel more attached to their home, independent of multiple socio-demographic factors such as income and gender (Evans et al, 2002).

For most of us, our accommodation is a key part of our physical environment. It frames our experiences of where we live and is therefore central to our sense of belonging to a town, village, city or other territory. This is particularly true for specialist retirement housing, such as retirement villages and extra care housing, which have very clear physical boundaries and are usually developed with the intention of working as a 'community'. This has important considerations for the development of a sense of community in housing with care settings, which will be discussed in Chapter Six.

It could be argued that the use of the term 'community' by government, among others, often appears to be based on some lost idyll of English village life, characterised by harmony and altruism. Hoggett (1997) points out that communities are a complex mix of multiple identities, networks and interests, a fact that policy makers often ignore. However, this is to some extent recognised in a recent emphasis in UK policy on promoting 'mixed' communities. For example, a report by the Urban Task Force included a recommendation that communities should be mixed in terms of tenure, income and ethnicity (Rogers, 1999: 11). This agenda was taken forward in the Sustainable Communities Plan (Office of the Deputy Prime Minister [ODPM], 2003b), which identifies a number of key features of sustainable communities, including fairness, tolerance, cohesion, respect and engagement with people from different backgrounds, cultures and beliefs. Housing can contribute to this mix in two main ways, according to this plan: by encouraging sustainability and by promoting social inclusion.

The fundamental belief behind these policies is that socially inclusive communities founded on diversity of housing are desirable and can be cohesive. This raises the question of whether tenure mix is an end in itself or a way to achieve greater income mix. Atkinson and Kintrea (2000) identified four categories of benefit from tenure/income mix: economic and service impacts, community-level effects, social and behavioural effects and overcoming social exclusion. Kearns and Mason (2007) suggest there is a broad aim to achieve greater social integration of diverse and advantaged/disadvantaged groups. At the same time, tenure mix is seen as a way of breaking up housing-based neighbourhoods with high levels of anti-social behaviour, which is why mixed community policies tend to be applied to deprived areas undergoing regeneration. However, much of the evidence for mixed communities comes from studies carried out in the US, and the evidence from Europe is much weaker. For example, a review of the literature by Kleinhans (2004) found little evidence of social interaction across tenures. Much of the evidence is mixed. For example, while one study of housing estates in Notting Hill supported mixed tenure as a way of promoting social mixing (Page and Boughton, 1997), another that explored a mixed-tenure retirement village found little evidence of cross-tenure social interaction (Evans and Means, 2007). It is worth noting here that the differences between designed and naturally occurring mixed communities could be a factor.

The relationship between tenure mix and social cohesion appears to be complex. Kearns and Mason (2007) found that, while the level of social renting is the most important determinant of incidence of anti-social behaviour, balanced communities in terms of tenure do not necessarily reduce neighbourhood problems, and social renting can offer satisfactory, quiet environments. It can also be argued that mixed tenure might have adverse effects, including feelings of envy and inferiority among lower-income households. Robertson et al (2008) supported diversity of housing type and tenure within a single neighbourhood as a way of preventing the creation of ghettoes, which can have a great cost for society and individuals. However, there is a dichotomy here in that they also found evidence that the greater the social distance the harder it is to create a sense of local identity. This supports other studies that found little social interaction across tenures (Evans and Means, 2007).

Whatever the strength of the evidence, a range of UK government strategies, including the National Strategy for Neighbourhood Renewal (Social Exclusion Unit, 2000) and the New Deal for Communities (ODPM, 2003a), aim to promote mixed communities. In addition, local planners are encouraged to create diversity by ensuring that all new housing developments and communities have a proportion of affordable/social-rented homes.

2.6 Conclusion

This chapter has explored the concept of community and how it has influenced social policy in the UK. Despite the continued promotion of community as a force for social cohesion, it is extremely difficult to define. Most theories of community have focused to varying degrees on three key elements: place attachment, shared interests and a sense of identity. For many people, social interaction is at the heart of a sense of community, and theorists have reflected this via concepts of social networks and social capital. Recently, theories of community have argued that the importance of geographical place is decreasing as a factor in a sense of community and that people's social networks are far more diverse than they used to be. This trend has been attributed to a range of factors, including greater social mobility, globalisation and the growth of the internet. It has also been suggested that shared interests and identities are increasingly important factors in a sense of community. For example, religious belief, ethnic background and leisure pursuits have all been identified as more important for defining characteristics of community than place.

In the UK the New Labour government has placed the concept of community at the centre of a range of policies and initiatives that aim to promote moral good and social order. However, many writers have dismissed this form of communitarianism as romanticised, authoritarian and an attempt to avoid any blame for social problems. It also appears to be based on a perception of communities as necessarily socially cohesive units. This assumption has been widely challenged on the grounds that communities can also be oppressive and conformist, and often include considerable amounts of conflict. This idea is developed by Taylor (2003), who talks about community as having a 'dark as well as a good side' because of its power as a force for exclusion as much as for membership. Much of the ambiguity that surrounds debates about 'community' lies in the way the term has often been used to describe both 'social space' and 'a collective consciousness of social connection' (Gilleard et al, 2007). In this chapter I have also compared the concept of community with that of neighbourhood.

This chapter has argued that physical place or neighbourhood remains a key element of many communities because, despite the impact of globalisation and other social changes, it provides the venues for those everyday social interactions that are central to a sense of community. This approach, which can be characterised as a theory of 'community in place', acknowledges the role of the built environment in developing and sustaining a sense of community. The design of housing and the public spaces around it is crucial, both in terms of its impact on social interaction among residents and its role in our sense of identity, belonging and attachment. New housing developments have the potential to include a range of design features that aim to support the development of a sense of community. These offer benefits for older people in particular, because these people are often disadvantaged by inaccessible design in mainstream housing and as a result can feel marginalised and isolated from the communities in which they live.

In the next chapter I consider how our experience of communities changes over the lifecourse and into older age, along with the implications of these changes for housing aspirations in later life.

THREE

Community and ageing

3.1 Introduction

This chapter focuses on how ideas and experiences of community change across the lifecourse and explores what current and future cohorts of retirees might want from their neighbourhood environment. Length of residence has often been closely linked with a sense of community and continuity of identity. However, a range of societal changes such as globalisation, increased mobility (social, geographical and occupational) and weakening intergenerational links are having an effect on the meaning and role of community. This chapter first explores how these changes affect older people. I suggest that community continues to be important, but that dissatisfaction with the extent to which modern society is meeting the needs of older people has led those who can to look for new settings. Some theories of community and ageing are considered, particularly in terms of place attachment and maintaining a sense of identity in later life. The next section explores the meaning of home to residents of housing with care schemes. In addition, the role of shared interests and features of the built environment in promoting community involvement for older people is considered. Finally, I discuss some of the reasons why many older people seek new-style communities in housing with care settings rather than choosing to age in place.

3.2 The importance of community and belonging for older people

Despite the best intentions of government through strategies such as Opportunity Age (Department for Work and Pensions [DWP], 2005) there is evidence to suggest that older people in the UK are becoming lonelier, more depressed and less satisfied with their quality of life (Allen, 2008). This is particularly the case for those who are poor, disabled, living alone or in rundown neighbourhoods. The demographics of population growth suggest that this situation is likely to become more problematic in coming years. For example, it has been estimated that by 2025 the number of people over 85 with a disability will double (Jagger et al, 2006), while increasing numbers of older people will be living alone. A number of factors can be identified that support wellbeing for this age group, with community participation and social interaction being among the most important. Access to social support, particularly in the form of close relationships, has been linked to increased quality of life, lower rates of depression and a greater ability to deal with stressful life events (for example Prince et al, 1998; Sugisawa et al, 2002; Godfrey et al, 2004).

The quality of older people's housing is a crucial factor in their wellbeing; poor housing can lead to depression as well as ill health. It is of great significance therefore that, despite some improvements in recent years, 34% of older people live in non-decent homes (Lee, 2006) and 13% live in homes that are in serious disrepair (ODPM, 2006).

The concept of 'home' is also important, particularly in terms of maintaining a sense of identity (Phillipson, 2007). This may be because, as Rubinstein and Parmelee (1992) suggest, one's home and possessions, as primary territories, are more easily controlled than public territories and are therefore given greater personal meaning. As shown in Chapter Two, early studies tended to emphasise 'place' as the crucial factor in a sense of community belonging, largely based on local social networks and sources of informal support. More recently the focus has moved to common interests and shared lifestyles as the 'glue' that binds communities together. This change has widely been attributed to globalisation and increased social mobility. According to Putnam (2000) this has resulted in reduced local social capital and the disengagement of individuals and families from a stable place-based community existence.

Gilleard and Higgs (2000) suggested that these changes have led many of us to be part of multiple communities in different physical settings. This is not to deny the powerful role of the spatial in the creation of ageing identities but it does mean that more people are able to make conscious choices about where they want to live and the lifestyle they want to adopt. This has led to what Savage et al (2005) call 'elective belonging', whereby places of residence (and work, and so on) are chosen to reflect and affirm self-identities, rather than on the basis of long-term place ties. This idea of the experience of belonging becoming detached from that of a fixed or defined community is also discussed by King et al (2000) in their study of English people retiring to Mediterranean countries as a way of announcing or reaffirming their identities in later life.

3.3 Community across the lifecourse

It would seem, then, that a sense of community is a crucial factor in quality of life for many older people. But how do experiences and perceptions of community change as people grow older? It has been suggested that each individual has a dynamic relationship with the meaning of community that is constantly evolving as a living process (Rowles, 1983). In this context, a number of factors are likely to influence the ways in which we experience and perceive a sense of community as we grow older. First, there is a body of evidence to suggest that the present generation of older people are more likely to have lived in the same community for most of their lives than future generations will have done. Second, older people tend to spend more time in their immediate neighbourhood than younger people and are therefore more likely to derive a strong sense of emotional attachment from their home and local surroundings. There is also evidence to suggest that for people aged 65 and over neighbours tend to also be good friends whom they socialise with, while for younger groups neighbourhood is not necessarily about social interaction but more to do with a sense of belonging and casual 'head nodding' (Marsh, 2006).

Rowles (1983) found a direct relationship between attachment to place and wellbeing, particularly for older people who have low mobility and tend to live in the same place for a long time. He identified three elements of attachment – physical, social and autobiographical 'insideness' – all of which are intimately related to a sense of self. In this respect, places come to represent a 'scrapbook', documenting the achievements of a lifetime. It is logical to conclude, therefore, that for older people, attachment is likely to be grounded in lifelong familiarity with a single setting, while for younger people there is less attachment to a specific physical environment. Giuliani and Feldman (1993) suggested that people–place bonds increase as people grow older and are stronger for women than men. They also reported that younger people are more attached to the city and middle-aged people to the home, while older people tend to be attached at all levels.

Several studies have suggested that a sense of belonging and identity is not static but that it changes over time and has varying degrees of intensity at different moments in each person's life. For example, Robertson et al (2008) concluded that social identities on housing estates are complex and dynamic, incorporating elements of both change and continuity. Hay (1998) placed the development of a sense of place over a person's lifetime in the context of broader human developmental processes. He suggested that in modern Western society the places to which people become attached change as a result of residential mobility. Therefore, people often develop bonds to types of places, such as the suburbs or rural settings, rather than to specific places. In this respect generic characteristics of place that affirm individual identities and lifestyles can be transferred from one specific location to another. Other writers have emphasised the importance of places other than residence across the lifecourse, including recreational and work settings (Shumaker and Taylor, 1983). Hay's case-study research in rural New Zealand communities found a strong correlation between intensity of sense of place and age. From this work he developed a framework of stages in the development of a sense of place over the lifecourse. According to this model, sense of place is particularly intense for the older old, whose levels of mobility and community participation tend to have decreased. A sense of place is of greater importance to this age group than to any other and is often based on reminiscence and the reinterpretation of life events.

Environmental gerontologists have also suggested that age brings an increased attachment to place as well as increased sensitivity to the social and physical environment. For example, a study of people living in ageing buildings (Ng et al, 2005) found that environmental factors closest to the home of the residents (quality of dwelling and neighbours) exerted a greater influence than more distant features of the wider community. This theme is also evident in the UK

National Strategy for Housing in an Ageing Society (DCLG, 2008) through the concept of 'lifetime neighbourhoods'. There is also an emphasis on the increasing importance of neighbourhoods as we age, particularly in terms of the need to create environments that are enabling and age proofed. The strategy identifies the role of the immediate built environment in terms of promoting health and wellbeing, providing access to services and facilities, supporting diversity and, crucially, enabling integration with the local community. The strategy is to be congratulated for its recognition of the need to reconnect housing with a system that has for so long focused on health and social care as the main contributors to quality of life and wellbeing, but it also raises questions about how sustainable such neighbourhoods can remain in the light of the ongoing closure of many local services, such as post offices, general practices, shops and banks. These are, after all, the very services on which older people rely, both as venues for social interaction and as resources to support their independence.

At the same time, the strategy included the aim to make 'Lifetime Homes' compulsory for public housing by 2011. This standard incorporates 16 criteria for creating accessible and adaptable housing in order to increase independence, choice and longevity of tenure. These relate to a range of interior and exterior features, including width of car parking spaces, approach gradients, communal stairs and lifts, wheelchair accessibility, bathroom layout and entrance-level bedspace. However, the fact that this standard was not to be compulsory for private housing does severely restrict its potential to benefit most older people. This is in spite of calculations that the additional cost of building homes to the lifetime standard are relatively minor (Sangster, 1997).

The World Health Organization (WHO) has also acknowledged the importance of the design of the built environment to older people through its Age-Friendly Cities initiative (WHO, 2006). By considering a range of factors, including outdoor spaces and buildings, transport, housing, employment, social participation, respect and health services, this initiative aims to promote supportive and enabling urban environments. The overall philosophy of this approach is that older people should be seen not as a burden but as a resource for families, communities and economies.

There is much evidence, then, to indicate that neighbourhood and a sense of community are of increasing significance as we grow older. At the same time, a considerable body of research suggests that many older people today feel less connected with their local area than they were in the past. For example, participants in a national consultation (Watts, 2008) highlighted the decline of community as one of the greatest 'social evils' in Britain today. In particular, it was felt that older people are increasingly isolated from their neighbours and that as a result of greed and selfishness people no longer see themselves as part of a wider community. To some extent this supports suggestions that community is becoming less place based, although it should be pointed out that the decline of community is a recurrent theme in social commentaries at least since the times of the Romans. Other findings included a perception of Britain as more dangerous and violent than in the past and a feeling among older participants that younger people were the main perpetrators of social evils such as anti-social behaviour. Revealingly, one older woman related the story of how she came across a group of young people standing around and was about to go the other way when she realised that it was her son and his friends. This demonstrates how ingrained the fear of young people has become among some older people, perhaps fuelled by a media focus on the negative aspects of youth in general, what we might call the 'hoodie' mentality.

Interestingly, older people who took part in this survey spoke about how different things used to be, with one saying that community had 'broken down' during the past 20 or 30 years. While such feelings could be said to demonstrate the nostalgia for imagined communities that many writers have referred to, they also lend support to the evidence suggesting that looking for a sense of community is one of several reasons that older people give for moving into housing with care schemes.

Several studies reinforce this suggestion that being part of a community is important to the people who live in retirement housing and was in many cases one of the reasons for moving there. In their review of the research literature, Croucher et al (2006) reported that retirement villages include key facilities that offer opportunities for social interaction and the development of a sense of community. They concluded that the overall attraction of such settings to older people was the combination of independence, security, social engagement and an active lifestyle. Bernard et al (2004) highlighted three main reasons for moving into Berryhill retirement village: autonomy, security and sociability. Similarly, Evans and Means (2007) provided a list of the most commonly reported reasons for moving into the retirement village that they studied. Feelings of isolation or loneliness, which suggests an element of searching for a sense of belonging, came fifth on the list, after their own health needs, proximity to family members, their partner's health needs, and difficulty managing the house or garden. The study included use of the How is Your Home? questionnaire, an adaptation of the Housing Options for Older People appraisal assessment tool used by the Elderly Accommodation Counsel (Heywood et al, 2001). Results indicated that the majority of residents felt social factors to be more important to them than physical ones in terms of overall levels of satisfaction with where they lived. High scores were also reported for security and human contact as important to quality of life. As might be expected, the reasons for moving into retirement housing are complex, but many people appear to be searching for social interaction and what might be loosely called a sense of community, however that might be defined.

3.4 Ageing and community in housing with care settings

I have presented a range of evidence to suggest that for many residents perceived opportunities for social interaction and a sense of community belonging are key factors in their decision to move into retirement housing. It is somewhat fortuitous therefore that many features of such environments have been shown to support the development of place attachment for older people. The increased importance of the immediate neighbourhood is of particular relevance here, because the majority of such schemes are new build and therefore incorporate features that make them accessible. However, it has also been shown that length of residence is associated with increased place attachment; it has been suggested that the main reason for the importance of length of residence is that changes in attachment to place across the lifecourse mirror stages of psychological development, so that our sense of identity and self-esteem become closely entwined with our sense of belonging to places and our interactions with the people with whom we share those places.

This would appear to present a major challenge to the wellbeing of people moving into housing with care settings, particularly in the light of the finding by Sugihara and Evans (2000) that the development of attachment to place and the formation of strong social ties are a prerequisite for successful transition to a retirement community. It can be argued that those living in housing with care settings have considerable control, or at least a feeling of control, over their environment, compared with many other settings. Indeed, this may be one of the main attractions of retirement villages, that living there offers older people the opportunity to choose and shape communities that are consistent with their own biographies and life histories. However, this means that those people for whom such choices are not available can end up feeling alienated and excluded due to the changes that take place in the neighbourhoods where they have aged, changes over which they feel they have little control.

The experiences of living in retirement housing can also be explored in relation to a range of theories of community. For example, the popularity of such environments supports the suggestion by some commentators that, for most people, shared interests are now more important than long-held place attachment to a sense of community (see for example Gilleard and Higgs, 2000). The attraction of housing with care settings is also interesting in the context of Pahl's (1970) theory of 'communities of the mind', whereby all communities are an illusion that we adopt in order to create a feeling of control and autonomy over our lives. It is, as Phillipson (2007) notes, important to make sense of older people's nostalgia for past 'imagined' communities, and this can be related to work by Biggs et al (2001), who suggested that the most important element of a sense of community is how residents perceive and experience themselves as part of a community. According to this interpretation, the 'community' label is applied to retirement housing settings so enthusiastically, largely because residents have such a strong psychological need for it to be a community. It is also, of course, attractive to the developers as a marketing 'tag' that helps them to make sales. In order to create and maintain this perception, the residents create stories that hold these 'communities' together in the minds of those who live there. These are what Papadopoulos (1999) called 'shared narratives', based on common experiences and identities. They also relate closely to Anderson's 'imagined communities' (1991). If it is the case that retirement housing schemes are experienced as communities only because the residents want and believe them to be so, the physical characteristics of these settings as places of residence are less important than the internal meanings they have for residents. For Biggs et al (2001) this leads to the conclusion that the success of retirement communities lies in their ability to 'create a secure and convincing narrative for identity in later life' (p 653). They call this 'a lifestyle of belief'. In addition, membership of a community only makes sense in relation to the existence of non-members who are, by definition, excluded. Maintaining this belief therefore depends on the identification of these non-members who do not enjoy the same sense of community wellbeing. In the retirement village studied by Biggs et al (2001) this took the form of stories about the inferior quality of life experienced by people in local neighbourhoods and nursing homes.

The concept of 'home' is another important aspect of feelings of attachment and belonging in housing with care. One of the distinctive characteristics of these settings is a focus on promoting independence by supporting people in their own houses or apartments. Residents all have their own front doors and enjoy the legal right to enjoy their own space as owners or tenants. This is contrasted with other settings such as care homes, which have characteristics that make them more institutional and less domestic. There is a considerable literature from a range of disciplines that explores the meaning of 'home'. For example, the sociologist Despres (1991) identified a range of psychological functions of home, including security and control, a refuge from the outside world, an indication of personal status and a reflection of personal values. Several writers have explored the meaning of 'home' for older people in particular, concluding that it is an integral part of personal identity and central to place attachment (see for example Askham and Hancock, 1999; Pastalan and Barnes, 1999). This role of home in maintaining continuity of personal identity in later life is reflected in the desire by many residents to incorporate their personal possessions into their retirement accommodation. This has been explored by Eshelman and Evans (2002), who discussed the design challenge of creating spaces that anticipate and celebrate personal possessions.

In their study of housing decisions in later life, Clough et al (2004) emphasised the importance of home for older people as a venue for social interaction and for providing privacy and a sense of control. They also found that some of the most common factors in decisions to move were fear of crime, money worries, a desire for independence and concerns about their status in society. These are also some of the main reasons given by older people for moving into extra care housing and retirement villages, a theme that I will return to in Chapter Six. Gurney and Means (1993) suggest that the meaning of home is in a constant state of change. This idea is supported by the finding of Askham and Hancock (1999) that disability, divorce and widowhood can counteract the positive aspects of home ownership, such as security, independence and identity, to the extent that it becomes a burden. This is particularly interesting in the context of housing with care, where reducing the burden of home ownership in the community is another of the reasons frequently given for moving in.

3.5 Conclusion

This chapter has reviewed some of the evidence to suggest that the current generation of older people feel nostalgic for a lost sense of community. It may be that the communities people feel they were once part of are as much imagined as they are real, but to a large extent this distinction is irrelevant. Either way, this seeking for a new community to belong to is one of the main motivations for those who move into housing with care settings. It is certainly an aspiration that developers tap into and place at the centre of their marketing strategies. It also reflects subtle changes in concepts of community for this group of older people. Rather than depending on longstanding attachment to a specific place, other factors have become more important to the development of place attachment and a sense of community belonging. In particular, shared interests and similar lifestyle aspirations are central to the identity of housing with care schemes as modern communities. Equally significant is the fact that a sense of community is promoted as an important and positive attribute of such settings. This feeling of being a member of something 'special' that not everyone is able to enjoy seems to feed the perception among residents that they really are part of a community. It also emphasises the fact that moving into a new environment in later life is not an option for everyone. Many older people cannot afford to purchase an apartment in a retirement village and there is currently very little rented accommodation of this type. Extra care housing is more of an option for people without significant assets; indeed, much of the existing extra care provision is only available for older people who are eligible for support with their care needs, and although some of the newer schemes include some apartments for sale, demand currently far exceeds supply.

It can also be argued that retirement villages have a number of characteristics that make them more attractive than extra care housing as somewhere to rediscover community. In particular, their size provides economies of scale that allow for the provision of a much greater range of facilities and amenities around which to build a community identity. However, these differences between retirement villages and extra care housing schemes are likely to become blurred as more not-for-profit organisations move into this sector and new models of provision continue to emerge. For example, there has been a recent growth in extra care villages that are on a similar scale to retirement villages while also including a greater proportion of properties for rent and affordable housing.

The growing popularity of housing with care schemes as new communities raises the question of why those who move there have given up on their previous accommodation in this respect. To put it another way, what is it about the areas where they were living beforehand that meant they were no longer working as communities for older people? The evidence from surveys and studies of the views of older people suggests that many feel that mainstream society is increasingly failing to meet their needs and aspirations in many ways. In particular, despite the contribution that older people can make to their local neighbourhood, there are many barriers that have been found to inhibit them from fully doing so. These include fear of crime, inadequate transport, poor design, lack of disabled access and insufficient information (Social Exclusion Unit, 2000). Taken together, these factors can lead to older people feeling excluded, alienated and detached from their local communities.

Although there is now a recognition that we should take the needs of older people more into account in terms of neighbourhood design, progress has been slow. It is not therefore surprising that those who have the opportunity to do so look elsewhere for their needs to be met. Housing with care environments, which have been specifically designed to meet the needs of older people and are actively portrayed as communities, are an obvious alternative. Many of the characteristics of these settings aim to address the concerns expressed by older people by including accessible design, promoting security and providing appropriate facilities nearby. In Chapters Four and Five I look at the characteristics of housing with care in more detail, both in the UK and internationally. Chapter Six then goes on to explore the extent to which these settings can deliver on their claim to be communities.

FOUR

Housing with care communities in the UK

4.1 Introduction

Providing sufficient housing for older people has become a policy priority in recent years, largely as a result of the rapid ageing of the population. The figures have been frequently quoted but they are worth summarising here because of their importance for the provision of both housing and care.

- The UK population aged over 65 grew by 31% from 7.4 million to 9.7 million between 1971 and 2006, while the number of people aged 85 and over grew by 69,000 from 2005 to 2006, reaching a record 1.2 million.
- The fastest-growing age group in the population is that of those aged 80 years and over, who currently constitute 4.5% (2,749,507) of the total population.
- By 2040, the number of people over 64 in Britain is expected to grow from 9.5 million to 15 million.

These trends will continue during the first half of this century as the large numbers of people born after the Second World War and during the 1960s baby boom grow older.

UK government policy has for many years supported older people to live in their own homes as a preferred option rather than moving into residential care. Residential care homes in particular have been seen as the last resort, largely because of their institutional image and a widespread belief that they are not conducive to independence. At the same time, traditional forms of sheltered housing are increasingly felt to be failing to meet the aspirations of the current generation of older people and have become 'hard to let' in some areas. This policy of 'ageing in place' has been challenged on various grounds, including the large number of older people living in poor-quality housing (Means, 2007) and the high prevalence of loneliness among older people who live alone in the community (Dalley, 2002). At the same time, much general housing is not suitable for older people who need care and there is a lack of appropriate services for older people who want to be cared for at home. In 2008 approximately 10% of people aged 65 or over were living in residential options such as nursing care homes, sheltered housing and extra care housing.

A variety of factors have led to a decrease in the number of residential care and nursing homes during recent years, including rising costs resulting from regulation of the labour market, increasing care standards and wage inflation. The UK National Strategy for Housing in an Ageing Society (DCLG, 2008) acknowledged the role of housing in health and wellbeing and highlighted the importance of integrating housing with health and social care. It also emphasised the need to build homes and neighbourhoods that are suitable for people as they grow older. To this end it set a timetable for making Lifetime Home Standards compulsory in all publicly funded housing by 2013. These standards aim to provide enabling environments and incorporate a level of future proofing. The features of lifetime homes will be explored in greater detail in Chapter Six, along with the concept of lifetime neighbourhoods. This present chapter explores two types of housing for later life that have become increasingly popular in recent years particularly as alternatives to traditional care homes: retirement villages and extra care housing.

4.2 The history of retirement villages and extra care housing

Retirement villages have existed in the UK in some form for hundreds of years. The first ones were probably established in Roman times, when they provided housing for retired soldiers in an attempt to reduce the number of unemployed veterans returning to their home country. In the early 1900s one of the first 'new-style' retirement villages to be built was Whiteley Village in southeast England. This scheme was built for 'aged poor persons' as a condition of the will of the owner of a large department store. Further villages were constructed in the 1950s, largely as groups of privately owned residences for retired older people in relatively good health who were able to live independently. Since then the number of retirement villages has increased rapidly with both not-for-profit organisations and private developers entering the sector. It is difficult to determine the overall number of retirement villages that have been built in the UK, largely because there is no agreed definition. One indication of numbers comes from a guide published in October 2008 by the Elderly Accommodation Counsel.[1] This lists 76 housing developments for older people that were described by their developers/managers as retirement villages.

Some of the difficulties of definition emerge from the fact that the nature of retirement communities has broadened in recent years and many now offer a range of options, including apartments for independent living, extra care housing, 'hotel-style' suites, nursing care homes and specialist dementia care services. Many villages also offer a range of tenure options, including private ownership, shared ownership and rented social housing, and provide extensive facilities and social and recreational activities. Flexible care is typically available, including home help, personal care, health care, home maintenance, eating facilities and transport. In marketing terms, retirement villages portray images of communities of 'like-minded' people enjoying a lifestyle based on visions of successful ageing and an active, worry-free retirement. Extra care housing is a more emergent form of provision that has developed during the last 20 years or so and has become established as another very popular model of specialist housing with care provision for older people in the UK. It also forms an important element of government policy in terms of its aims to promote choice, independence and wellbeing for older people.

4.3 Defining extra care housing and retirement villages

Extra care housing and retirement villages are described in detail in sections 4.4 and 4.5 below. However, it is important first to summarise what they are and how they differ from each other. This is not an easy task because both are evolving rapidly as models with a wide range of variants, making it difficult to offer accurate generic descriptions. Some of the models that have been developed are described later in this chapter. Distinctions between extra care housing and retirement villages are rather blurred. Both aim to provide environments that are lively, sociable and of a high build specification, in which both fit and frail older people (usually aged 55 or over) can live independently, while offering care and support services when needed. For residents who are able to carry out basic activities of daily living, care and support services can be provided in their own homes, usually up to a maximum number of hours per week. If care is required beyond that level the resident may need to move into a care home setting, either on site or nearby. Most schemes accommodate people with early-stage dementia. Some schemes include dementia units in which residents can continue to live as their disease progresses, while in others people with dementia often have to move out because staff and other residents struggle to cope with some aspects of their behaviour.

Despite these difficulties of definition, the two types of provision do share several key characteristics as follows:

- the availability of high levels of care;
- 24-hour onsite care staff;
- an extensive range of facilities;
- residency is age restricted, often to those aged 55 and over.

Table 4.1 (taken from Evans et al, 2008) provides a useful summary of the key features of extra care housing, retirement villages and some other forms of specialist accommodation for later life.

Table 4.1: Models of housing with care and residential care

	Extra care housing	Retirement village	Sheltered housing	Residential care
Also known as	Very sheltered housing; category 2.5; integrated housing with care; close care.	Continuing care retirement village; retirement community.	Category 1, 1.5, or 2; retirement housing court; supported housing.	Category 3; care home; rest home; elderly mental infirm (EMI) unit; nursing home.
Key features	Typically 40 or more self-contained flats with ensuite facilities. Fully wheelchair accessible and inclusive design standards. Some schemes have 'specialist clusters' of flats for people with dementia.	100 or more houses, apartments or bungalows. Many have a care home on site; a few have dementia units.	Typically clusters of 30–40 flats, bedsits or bungalows; mostly self-contained; designed to meet accessibility standards.	Residential care homes typically have a number of rooms, some with private bathrooms and kitchenettes, onsite catering facilities and resident lounges.
Provided by	Mostly housing associations, some local authorities. Increasingly private sector developers are building extra care 'villages'.	Not-for-profit organisations, housing associations and private developers.	Local authorities, housing associations (social rented), and some private developers.	Mostly local authorities and private care companies.
Tenure options	Social renting, shared ownership, outright sale and mixed tenure. Assured tenancy rights.	Some for private ownership, some mixed tenure (private ownership, shared ownership and renting). Assured tenancy rights.	Much stock is social rented, but new build is for outright sale or leasehold. Assured tenancy rights.	Most 'placements' are paid for by local authorities or privately. No tenancy rights.
Typical facilities	Communal lounge; catering; shop; beauty salon; day centre; activities room; internet room.	Communal lounge; catering; shop; activities room; beauty salon; internet room; gym; swimming pool; jacuzzi.	Communal lounge; laundry.	Communal lounges; catering.
Care and support	Emergency alarm system; 24-hour onsite care and support (including at least one 'waking carer' during the night).	Emergency alarm system. Most have flexible packages that can be purchased from care team and out-of-hours emergency provision.	Emergency alarm system. Most have onsite or visiting warden. Residents can access domiciliary care in the same way as anyone living in their own home.	Onsite care staff 24 hours a day, 7 days a week. Registered with Commission for Social Care Inspection.
Provision in England	30,000 units in 2006.	Not known.	500,000 units in 2006.	476,200 registered care home places in 2005.

It is also possible to identify two significant ways in which extra care housing and retirement villages often differ. The first of these is the nature of care provision. Although both offer housing and a range of care options, most (though not all) extra care residents have some form of care package, while many of those living in retirement villages receive no care at all. This is because some people move into retirement villages soon after or even before they retire and continue to live there independently for many years. The second difference is in terms of scale. Extra care schemes usually range in size from a few bungalows to over 50 flats. Retirement villages, on the other hand, tend to contain over 100 units of housing, with the largest in the UK now approaching about 600 units. This allows retirement village developers to achieve economies of scale and provide a wider range of facilities and services than is usually available in extra care housing. However, even this distinction is becoming less meaningful as a new range of extra care villages is being built. These provide many of the features of housing and care often found in extra care schemes but on the scale of retirement villages.

Having given a flavour of what these two forms of housing provide, this chapter will now explore extra care housing and retirement villages in more detail and look at how they have developed in the UK.

4.4 Extra care housing

The first forms of extra care housing emerged in the 1980s, when housing providers adapted traditional sheltered housing to include additional facilities and services. These models were widely known as 'category two and a half', falling as they did between category 2 sheltered housing and category 3 residential homes. The potential for this hybrid form of housing to support the needs of an ageing population was widely recognised during the 1990s, at which time it became known as 'very sheltered housing' and more recently the term 'extra care housing' came into common use. However, because extra care housing has evolved in a number of ways across an increasing range of providers, it is also still known by several different names, including sheltered housing plus, housing with care, frail elderly housing, enhanced sheltered housing, assisted living and close care.

A 'typical' new-build extra care scheme, Priory Court, is described in Case Study One on page 36. However, this form of provision continues to evolve and there are now many different models of extra care housing in the UK. This flexibility makes it difficult to provide an accurate definition and there is no agreement as to exactly what it is. This book adopts the broad definition as used by the Department of Health Housing Learning and Improvement Network (LIN) (Riseborough and Fletcher, 2004). This definition focuses on philosophy and vision more than measurable characteristics and suggests the following three key attributes:

• being primarily housing and not an institution;
• supporting ageing in place and promoting independent living;
• sometimes incorporating services for intermediate care and rehabilitation.

Case Study One: Priory Court extra care scheme, Gateshead, England

Priory Court, which opened in 2002, is one of five extra care schemes that Housing 21 developed in partnership with Gateshead Borough Council. It is situated in a residential suburb close to Newcastle City Centre, surrounded by a mixture of council houses and new-built 'executive' housing. The court is built largely of brick and glass, giving it a light and spacious feel. Onsite facilities include a shop, restaurant, activities room and beauty salon, all of which are open to the public and are well used by people living nearby.

Priory Court provides 40 one-bed self-contained flats over two storeys. All residents are nominated by Gateshead Social Services and the scheme provides a maximum of care hours per week. Personal care services are provided by a team of onsite Housing 21 care staff and a part-time activities coordinator is also employed.

A number of common features of extra care housing can be identified. Another Housing LIN factsheet, 'Models of extra care and retirement communities' (King, 2004), lists the following range of key features:

- self-contained flats or bungalows – a defining feature;
- distinguishing extra care from residential care;
- provision of an appropriate package of care, in the individual's own accommodation, to a high level if required;
- dwellings incorporate design features and assistive technology to facilitate independence of frail older people and provide a safe environment;
- includes catering facilities with one or more meals available each day;
- 24-hour care staff and support available;
- more comprehensive and extensive communal facilities than sheltered housing, such as a restaurant, lounge(s), activity room(s), library, health suite, computer suite, consultation room and so on;
- includes onsite staff offices and facilities;
- domestic support services, including help with shopping, cleaning and possibly making meals;
- specialist equipment to help meet the needs of frail or disabled residents, for example: laundry, assisted bathing, sluice, hoist, also charging and storage facilities for electric wheelchairs/scooters;
- social and leisure activities/facilities and additional individual or shared services, such as a shop, hairdressing, chiropody, massage, alternative therapies, cash machine and a post box;
- mobility and access assistance, for example communal buggies or shared pool car.

As King points out, the first five or six items in this list are usually considered as essential to extra care housing, while the remainder can be found to varying degrees. In contrast, all of these features are usually found in retirement villages. Even comprehensive definitions such as this can be problematic, particularly as the nature of provision changes and adapts. For example, there are some smaller extra care schemes where catering facilities have become financially unviable and ready-prepared meals are brought in to be reheated in microwave ovens. The recent development of extra care 'villages', which include some of the characteristics of retirement villages, has made definitions even more difficult. One example is Hartfields in the north of England, which was developed by the Joseph Rowntree Foundation in partnership with Hartlepool Borough Council, Hartlepool Primary Care Trust and North Tees and Hartlepool NHS Trust. This large complex provides 242 apartments and cottages, a range of social activities and leisure facilities and care and support as needed. It sits on the edge of a new neighbourhood park and is designed to be part of a wider residential development.[2]

Another key feature of both extra care housing and retirement villages is that residents have the full legal rights associated with being a tenant or homeowner, unlike those living in residential and nursing care homes who have a licence to occupy the premises. Residents are therefore living in their own homes, and this is reflected in designs that aim not to look or feel in any way institutional. Extra care is primarily about 'quality of life' not just 'quality of care' (Riseborough and Fletcher, 2004), and promoting independence is a central component of this philosophy. The UK government has been particularly keen to promote the growth of extra care housing because supporting independence is at the heart of its strategies, such as the National Framework for Older People (Department of Health, 2001).

The Elderly Accommodation Counsel (EAC), a UK charity that aims to help older people make informed choices about meeting their housing and care needs, compiles statistics on the provision of extra care housing in England. At the beginning of 2008 it identified 935 schemes providing 39,141 housing units, 29,552 of them for rent, mostly from local authorities or registered social landlords, and the remainder for sale (EAC, 2008a). The EAC has also recently introduced a 'quality of information' mark, which aims to standardise the information available to people looking for retirement housing. This provides comprehensive scheme profiles, including details of the accommodation available, distances to local services, what services and facilities are provided, rental and sale costs, staffing, service-user profiles and culture/lifestyle. Although this does not solve the problem of defining extra care housing, it does at least make it much easier for service users and their family carers to compare one scheme with another and therefore to make an informed choice.[3]

4.4.1 Providing the housing and the care in extra care housing

Because extra care is essentially a form of housing provision, with people living in their own homes, any care that is provided is domiciliary care rather than residential care. The 2000 Care Standards Act created a new regulatory framework for all currently regulated social care and independent health care services. It identified the following four categories of care:

- non–physical care;
- emotional and psychological support;
- assistance with bodily functions such as feeding, bathing and toileting;
- care that just falls short of assistance with bodily functions but still involving physical and intimate touching, including activities such as helping a person get out of a bath and helping them to get dressed.

All four of these are commonly provided within extra care housing and the last two fall within the requirement for registration as care providers with the Commission for Social Care Inspection (CSCI). This means that the care provider must normally be registered with CSCI as a domiciliary care provider, although there are some exceptions. Being assessed as in need of a minimum number of hours of care is often, but not always, one of the eligibility and allocation criteria for extra care housing. Where extra care provides an element of social housing it is common for a panel of partner representatives to consider applications jointly. This panel comprises representatives from social services, the housing department, the housing provider and health services. The resident has a contract with the housing provider for the accommodation and related services, and a separate agreement covering the provision of care. This separation of housing and care services is crucial to the housing provider because it avoids the necessity to register extra care schemes as care homes, which would mean complying with additional regulations.

Exactly how care is provided within extra care housing varies and depends largely on the relationship between the following three parties in delivering the service:

- The housing provider, who is the landlord and sometimes also the developer of the scheme. This role includes housing management, low-level support (sometimes through a warden type of role), property maintenance and service-user involvement.
- The care provider, who can be a charity, a local authority, a private company or a housing association. They provide domiciliary care, more intensive personal care and sometimes also nursing care.
- Social services (sometimes known as adult and community care), who commission and fund services, and sometimes provide them, as well as assessing needs.

Care can be provided by these partners in four main ways:

- The housing and care are provided by the same organisation.
- The housing is provided by one organisation and the care by another, via a contract with social services.
- The housing is provided by one organisation and the care is provided directly by social services.
- The housing is provided by one organisation and the care is provided by multiple organisations, either via contracts with social services or through direct payments.

There are potential advantages and disadvantages to separating housing provision from care services, because a good housing provider is not necessarily the best care provider and vice versa. However, separating the services can present challenges to providing a seamless service to residents, leading to extra costs such as liaison and coordination. Although extra care housing residents are legally entitled to choose who their care provider is, so far the extent to which this has happened appears to be very limited. There are a number of advantages to using the on-site care team, including achieving economies of scale, better access to care in an emergency and increased coordination between housing and care services.

4.4.2 Tenure in extra care

The majority of extra care housing that is sponsored by local authorities is 100% rented and represents public sector housing provision for the less well-off. However, mixed tenure is becoming increasingly common, particularly in the larger extra care 'villages'. For example, many of the extra care schemes that are currently being developed by the Extra Care Charitable Trust offer options to buy, rent and share ownership. One of these, Lovat Fields village, is profiled in Case Study Two below. The mixed-tenure model is discussed in more detail in section 4.5 on retirement villages.

Case Study Two: Lovat Fields extra care village, Milton Keynes, England

Lovat Fields extra care village was developed by the Extra Care Charitable Trust in collaboration with Milton Keynes Council. It opened in 2007 and provides accommodation in 244 apartments and 14 bungalows. It is aimed at people aged 55 and over who are fit or frail, with a number of spaces reserved for people with care needs.

Three types of tenure are available:
- rent only;
- part purchase, allowing residents to purchase up to 75% of their property and rent the remainder;
- outright purchase.

All three options include the opportunity for residents to apply for support with their housing and care costs. Tenures are pepperpotted throughout the scheme and are not distinguishable from each other.

Onsite facilities include a lounge, dining room, restaurant, laundry, guest facilities, garden, conservatory, community centre, hobby room, activities room, cafe, shop, hairdressing salon, jacuzzi, bar/pub and a library.

Most schemes aim to achieve a mixture of fit and frail residents, largely as a way of promoting a 'balanced community'. However, many people need more care as they age, which means that, over time, more people are likely to move into the 'high dependency' category. This, along with increasing funding pressures, can stretch the resources for care and support provision. In some schemes, lettings are only available to people with higher-end care needs, in which case extra care is usually seen as a direct alternative to residential care. A holistic approach is usually taken when assessing need for extra care, looking at personal and family circumstances, current housing and support needs. In practice, many people move into extra care settings because of a crisis situation – such as a health emergency, accident, sudden illness or death of a partner – which significantly affects their ability to remain living independently in their homes.

4.4.3 The costs of extra care housing

The costs of developing extra care vary but can be considerable. It has been estimated that new-build development costs range from £50,000 to £70,000 per unit, while remodelling sheltered housing into extra care costs between £3,000 and £15,000 a unit, plus £3,000 to £11,000 per unit for developing communal areas. The majority of extra care housing built so far has been part funded by Housing Corporation and Department of Health grants, which provided £147 million of funding between 2004 and 2008. Much of this funding was awarded to registered social landlords (RSLs), including many housing associations. Private developers have now started to enter the retirement housing market, often using borrowed money to fund core costs and relying on sales and rental income to make repayments.

The services provided to people living in extra care housing are another important component in the costs of developing and running a scheme. King et al (2005) break these down into four categories: accommodation, housing management, support services and care services. These are commonly funded from a range of sources, including housing benefit, Supporting People funding, social services funding and residents' own income (which can include the use of attendance allowance and direct payments). The exact mix of funding depends on the nature of the scheme. For example, Supporting People operates in two main ways, depending on tenure. Where residents are renting, the Supporting People Administering Authority (SPAA) usually negotiates a contract with the provider for the entire scheme and carries out regular performance reviews in relation to standards of delivery. For leaseholders, however, each resident has to make an individual claim to the SPAA, which is increasingly insisting that the support services for new schemes are put out to tender. A further challenge for providers is that if the SPAA reduces funding then support services may have to be changed or even withdrawn.

The costs of providing care to extra care housing residents can be met from a range of sources. Where a scheme is providing social housing the care costs are usually funded by social services (sometimes known as adult and community care), often as a block contract for a standard number of hours per week. Health services provided within extra care schemes are usually provided by the local primary care trust. Residents are usually responsible for paying a care charge, along with housing-related costs such as rent and a service charge, which is based on the number of hours of care they receive. Some will qualify for subsidies after a financial assessment, while those who do not (self-funders) may qualify for attendance allowance and direct payments to cover some or all of this cost.

One of the key features of extra care housing is the inclusion of an onsite care team that operates 24 hours a day. Within this overall model there are a wide range of approaches to staffing, but most are based on a structure of a manager, senior carers and a team of care assistants. Care assistants are usually trained to NVQ level 2 and staff are predominantly female, with many working part time. Out-of-hours care is sometimes limited to 'sleeping cover' to deal with any emergencies that arise. There are some differences between providers in terms of staffing models. Some integrate the housing management and care management roles within a single person. Many follow a system whereby the staff team support each tenant across a range of needs, including personal care, domestic tasks and social activities, often on a key-worker basis. Others contract out care, cleaning and catering functions to separate agencies.

4.4.4 Recent developments in extra care housing in the UK

Extra care housing is an increasingly popular model of provision for older people and has become a key plank of government policy in terms of its aims to promote choice, independence and wellbeing for older people. This growth was initially informed by a government study that concluded that there was over-provision of conventional sheltered housing and insufficient extra care housing to meet demand (McCafferty, 1994). It also became apparent that some sheltered housing had become hard to let, largely because it was in poor condition and no longer met older people's aspirations and expectations for housing quality. For example, much sheltered housing provision was small, bedsit-style accommodation and some had shared bathrooms and/or toilets.

As a result of these factors, a considerable amount of government funding has been invested in extra care as a modern form of provision that meets the aspirations of today's older people. Extra care housing is provided by both the public and private sector, and many areas of the UK now have an older people's housing strategy that has been developed in collaboration with a range of agencies. These can include the local authority, social care, the primary care trust and the housing sector. The Gateshead Council strategy is a good example of this, as summarised in Case Study Three. National and regional requirements were established by the Housing Corporation, which also provided considerable public sector funding through the Social Housing Fund.

Case Study Three: Gateshead Council Housing Strategy for Older People 2007–12: a summary

'The Housing Strategy for Older People aims to rebalance the older persons' housing market, to ensure independence and social inclusion and make sure that older people have active and fulfilling lives within sustainable communities. It will work towards meeting the needs and aspirations of older people well into the future. It aims to provide more new accommodation, detail investment in existing housing across tenures, provide affordable housing and Lifetime Homes and provide more extra care accommodation. It is based on extensive stakeholder and service-user consultation as well as research that supports our understanding of what we need to do.
...

The four main objectives of this strategy are to:

- ensure that the housing options available to older people more closely meet their aspirations and create choice;
- support people to stay in their own home for longer;
- support independence and social inclusion;
- ensure that older people have access to warm and eco-friendly housing in safe and secure communities.

Gateshead Council's Housing Strategy for Older People 2007–12, Summary, available at www.gateshead.gov.uk/Housing/Strategy/PoliciesStrategies/home.aspx

---

In addition to development funding from the Housing Corporation, the government has invested or committed £227 million between 2004 and 2010 in the Extra Care Housing Fund, which is administered by the Department of Health. Its purpose is to fund and develop innovative new schemes or remodel existing sheltered housing or residential care schemes to deliver specific health outcomes. Funded schemes are required to contribute to the range of solutions aimed at preventing unnecessary admissions into hospital or residential care, and/or to assist in reducing delayed transfers of care from hospitals. Successful schemes from this investment programme also need to show how they deliver an inclusive approach for adults with long-term conditions, including learning difficulties, physical disabilities, dementia and mental health. One criticism of this form of housing with care is that it has developed partly in response to the availability of subsidy and local popularity, rather than by targeting resources to meet identified need (Means et al, 2003).

Although the majority of extra care housing has so far been developed by not-for-profit organisations, there is an increasing amount of private-sector provision, largely aimed at owner-occupiers. Private developers are eligible for extra care grants in partnership with local authorities, but so far most have instead preferred to borrow the capital required against the finished scheme. Once built, both sales and rental income from properties can be used to meet loan repayments. Residents usually buy a long lease and pay a service charge that covers repair and maintenance, the provision of a range of onsite staff, an emergency alarm system and a basic level of domestic assistance. Additional services can be purchased as required, such as meals and care and support packages. Private developers will often work with another organisation, either a private company or a housing association, that takes on day-to-day management of the scheme. In terms of care services, developers can either provide these services themselves, contract them out to a domiciliary care provider or create a partnership with the local social services department.

Extra care housing has usually been seen as fulfilling three main roles within a housing and care context:

- as a replacement for sheltered housing
- as an extension to sheltered housing
- as an alternative to residential care.

Many local authorities have adopted a strategy of replacing residential care home provision with extra care housing, partly due to a report from the Royal Commission on Long-Term Care, which concluded that it is both more cost effective and provides a better quality outcome for service users (Sutherland, 1999). An example of this approach comes from Hampshire, where in 2007/08 the county council closed six residential and nursing care homes because they felt that the ongoing repair costs were too high. The council calculated that refurbishing two of the care homes would cost £3.3 million, while closing them would save £1.8 million a year in running costs. At the same time, plans were announced to commission four new extra care housing schemes as a 'cheaper' alternative. However, such strategies have not been without opposition and it is important to recognise that care homes remain an important and preferred option for some older people. Another trend is for the remodelling of hard-to-let sheltered housing as extra care. However, this is far from simple and it may be that the oldest and least suitable stock that is suffering difficulties with letting is the least suitable for conversion. A study by Tinker et al (2007) identified a range of challenges for this approach, including the disturbance involved for existing residents of either moving temporarily or living in the middle of a building site. Crucially, they concluded that it cannot be assumed that remodelling is a cheaper option than new build. An interesting example of remodelling is provided by Callendar Court in Gateshead. This extra care scheme was formerly a tower block on a council estate and has been turned into a very successful and popular scheme, incorporating a range of facilities that are open to the local community. A summary of this scheme is presented in Case Study Four below.

Case Study Four: Callendar Court, Gateshead, England

Background

Callendar Court was a local authority tower block that has been remodelled to provide extra care housing on 11 storeys in 40 one- and two-bedroom flats. A major feature was the addition of a ground-floor extension that houses a range of facilities for use by residents and people in the local area.

Housing and care

Each of the ten storeys above the ground floor contains four flats with either one or two bedrooms, and two storeys also have a common room. Gateshead Council provide the care via a 24/7 community-based service while Housing 21, a provider of retirement housing, care and support services for older people, provides laundry and housework facilities. Non-resident management staff operate from offices on the ground floor.

Facilities

The new entrance opens into the facilities area, which houses a range of facilities that are open to residents and local people, including a lounge, cafe, lifts, laundry, guest room, hobby room, shop and hairdressing salon. It also contains the scheme offices, the kitchens, a wheelchair store and toilets. Callendar Court has two wheelchair-accessible flats, both of which are on the ground floor.

The facilities are well used by residents and people in the area, which is a close-knit community, and this helps to make it feel integrated with the estate on which it sits. Further facilities are available nearby, including bus stops (200 metres), a social centre (200 metres), a general store (400 metres), a post office (400 metres) and a general practice (800 metres). The nearest town centre is Gateshead, approximately 1 mile (1.5 kilometres) away.

Learning points

A wide range of factors need to be taken into account when remodelling any existing form of housing as extra care, including planning requirement, building standards and costs.

Consultation with all interested parties is crucial. Particular consideration should be paid to the views, needs and preferences of existing residents, including how they will be rehoused and/or the potential impact of the work on their living environment.

Any decisions to remodel should take full account of all appropriate existing strategies at district, county and regional levels, including those that specifically relate to older people and/or housing. Imaginative approaches to remodelling can transform unsatisfactory buildings into environments that support a good quality of life for residents.

In the current example, a hard-to-let tower block has become a popular extra care scheme that is integrated into the local area. A key factor in this success has been the addition of a ground-floor extension, which provides a range of facilities for residents and the local community.

Photo 1: Callendar Court in Gateshead: a council block remodelled as extra care housing

Source: This case study was initially commissioned by the Housing Learning and Improvement Network and can be found on their website at http://networks.csip.org. uk/IndependentLivingChoices/Housing/, along with a extensive range of resources in relation to housing with care.

More recently, new models of extra care housing have emerged, including those that serve as a base for services for the wider community, offer respite and intermediate care and provide specialist dementia care services. Given the extent to which extra care housing has changed since it first appeared, it is likely that further models will evolve.

4.4.5 The popularity of extra care housing

For many older people, forms of retirement housing such as extra care are preferable to residential care, largely because of the independence and opportunities for social interaction that they provide. A recent poll found that nine out of ten homeowners wanted to stay in their own home for the rest of their lives and two thirds feared being forced into a care home as they got older (Carvel, 2007). One significant advantage of retirement housing over traditional residential care is that it can enable couples to remain living together where one partner has a high level of care needs. In addition, if that person dies, the surviving partner is usually able to remain in their home if that is their choice, regardless of their care needs at the time. Affordability is another feature of extra care housing that can make it attractive to older people. Case Study Five below describes an example of shared ownership arrangements, which meant that some apartments were available in 2007 for as little as £47,500.

Case Study Five: Mere View, Suffolk, England

Mere View, an extra care housing development in Suffolk comprising 32 one- and two-bedroom apartments, was shortlisted in the 2007 Affordable Home Ownership Awards. All of the apartments were available on a 50% or 75% shared ownership basis, with prices starting at £47,500. This could enable residents to live mortgage free and/or release equity in their retirement. The scheme was a partnership between Housing 21, Housing Corporation, Mid-Suffolk District Council and Suffolk County Council. It was designed to fit in with its rural surroundings and with the aim of making it part of the village of Haughley by using traditional construction materials. In addition, design techniques were included to help people to navigate the building easily and safely, such as the use of colour to aid orientation. There are gardens that provide year-round interest and sensory experience. A range of features were incorporated in order to minimise environmental impact, such as under-floor heating and high levels of insulation.

Facilities include an onsite hairdressing salon and a cafe, both of which are open to the general public and the residents of an adjacent sheltered housing development. The village, which is approximately 400 metres away, offers a range of facilities, including a general store, a post office, a restaurant, a bakers and two public houses. There are also two churches, a football and social club, a bowls club and a gardening club.

It is estimated that there are currently 700,000 people with dementia in the UK and that this figure will increase to over 1 million people by 2025. The increasing prevalence of dementia therefore makes it a major consideration for housing provision, particularly in relation to a range of symptoms that can include loss of memory, confusion and problems with speech and understanding. Vallelly et al (2006) reported that extra care housing has considerable potential to support independence for people with dementia, although a range of factors need to be taken into account. These will be explored in more detail in Chapter Six in relation to the extent to which people with dementia can be part of a community in retirement housing settings.

Accessible design is another feature of extra care housing that makes it an attractive option for people who wish to retain their independence in later life. The majority of schemes are designed to be 'future proofed', so that they can be adapted to meet the needs of residents as they age. Features include kitchen units that can be lowered or raised, level-access showers, wiring for the fitting of warden alarms and strengthened ceiling joists to allow lifts and hoists to be fitted later. Despite the rapid growth of extra care housing it should not be viewed as a single solution to providing housing and care that meets the aspirations of all older people, but rather as one of many available choices.

4.5 Retirement villages

4.5.1 The main features of retirement villages

Retirement villages have been described as the 'third way' between living in the community and in a residential/nursing care home (Peace and Holland, 2001). This reflects an increasingly prevalent view of care homes as a last resort when all other options have been exhausted, largely as a result of an image of care homes as institutional and fostering dependency. This is an image that contrasts vividly with aspirations for empowerment, choice and autonomy on the part of the increasing number of older people. Retirement villages are usually self-contained developments that offer housing, care and support in an environment that aims to promote independence and offers a range of social and leisure activities. A range of tenures are commonly provided, including rental, outright purchase and shared ownership. Flexible care packages can be purchased by residents to meet their changing needs, and some retirement villages have onsite care homes. The main feature that differentiates them from extra care housing schemes is their size. For example, while most extra care housing schemes have up to 50 apartments, retirement villages are more likely to have about 200 units. There is a trend towards increasingly larger developments; one of the biggest is Middleton Towers in Lancashire, with up to 600 homes. With size come significant economies of scale, which mean that retirement villages commonly offer a wider range of facilities than extra care housing. For example Roseland Parc, a retirement village near

Truro in Cornwall, incorporates a comprehensive range of facilities and leisure opportunities, as outlined in Case Study Six.

Case Study Six: Roseland Parc retirement village, Truro, England

Roseland Parc is situated in a small village a few miles outside the town of Truro in Cornwall. It incorporates 59 cottages and apartments across two types of accommodation: independent living and fully serviced apartments. Care services are provided by an onsite care team, who also deliver care to older people in the local area. There is also a 36-bed care home for residents who need nursing as well as personal care. This facility can also support people with a physical disability or short-term memory loss and those who need end-of-life care.

The village is set in seven acres (three hectares) of wooded and landscaped grounds and has a wide range of facilities, including a shop, restaurant/bar, chapel, beauty salon, bowling green, boules court, palm garden and croquet lawn. There is also a spa that includes a heated swimming pool, a hot tub and a gym and stretching area. Regular exercise classes are held and both physiotherapy and complementary therapy services are available.

Retirement villages vary in respect of how their facilities are located within the development, with two main models being found:

- Core and cluster: a central building contains most of the communal facilities like a restaurant, library, reception, health suite and often a residential care home. People live in their own properties scattered around the core building and access services and facilities as they need them.
- Dispersed facilities: facilities are located in clusters throughout the site, based around smaller units of accommodation.

Retirement villages offer a range of financial options. Residents usually pay two types of fee: a one-off entry payment or weekly rental amount to cover the cost of the accommodation, and a regular annual or monthly fee for the duration of their stay. The entry fee is often substantial and covers the capital costs of construction, while the regular fee is much lower and covers maintenance, communal services and care support costs. The key point in some models is that, provided certain health criteria are satisfied on entry, the regular fee is partially or entirely independent of the level of care provided. If care is required on a long-term basis life savings will not be quickly depleted, as they would in a nursing home. This 'actuarial' model was adopted by Hartrigg Oaks, opened by the Joseph Rowntree Housing Trust in 1998 as one of the first continuing care retirement communities (CCRCs) in the UK; the scheme is profiled in Case Study Seven. This arrangement works in a similar way to an insurance scheme, whereby capital payments and annual fees from each resident are pooled to fund care and support services for all the residents. This means that an increased need for care does not lead to an increase in fees. The initial fee covers occupation of a bungalow and, if needed, a room in the onsite care home. Residents are encouraged to move in when they are fit and healthy and in the early stages of retirement. Applicants are required to take a health and care check and submit a financial statement. This scheme also aims to encourage residents of a range of ages in order to maintain a 'vibrant mixed community'. No upper age limit is set, but priority is given to the youngest applicants. Research by Croucher et al (2003) showed that this was a popular model because of the financial certainties that it offered to residents. However, there are considerable challenges to sustaining this model as the resident population ages and their care needs increase. As a result, most developments, such as Hartfields (see page 37 above), do not operate an actuarial model but instead offer a range of flexible care options that residents can buy into as their needs change.

Case Study Seven: Hartrigg Oaks, York, England

This is the first UK example of a continuing care retirement community financed through an insurance-based model, whereby residents pay an annual fee into a communal pool, which is used to fund the care and support needs of residents. The fee that residents pay therefore does not increase according to their use of care services. This model can only work if most residents do not make extensive use of the care and support services, which can be a challenge as the residents grow older.

The community is on a 21-acre (8.4-hectare) site two miles (three kilometres) from York city centre; it is for couples or single people aged 60 or over. There are 152 one- and two-bedroom bungalows, built to Lifetime Homea Standards, and a nursing care centre with 42 ensuite bedsitting rooms. Facilities include a restaurant, coffee shop, hairdressers, music room, health centre, community shop, library and computer room.

Three housing with care options are commonly provided within retirement villages. These can be described as independent living accommodation, fully serviced apartments and a nursing care home.

- *Independent living.* Residents buy an apartment and pay a monthly service charge. This usually covers external maintenance of the property, building insurance, window cleaning, provision of a vehicle and driver for external trips (in some villages this incurs an extra charge), satellite TV/internet access/telephone line rental, and maintenance of amenities and the grounds. A range of personal care services can also be purchased flexibly as residents' needs change.
- *Fully serviced apartments.* These are sold with a 'hotel-style' package of services and require the payment of a higher level of charge. In addition to the services provided for the basic service charge, residents who purchase this package also

receive a supply of breakfast provisions to be prepared in their kitchenette, two full meals a day (delivered to their home or eaten in a village restaurant), daily visits from a carer, a bedding and laundry service and access to personal care from the onsite domiciliary care team.

- *Nursing care home.* Some retirement villages incorporate a nursing care home that can support people who have a physical disability or short-term memory loss, or who are terminally ill. A range of care options are usually provided, including respite care, convalescence, short-term arrangements and care on a long-term basis. They often have close links with local health and pharmacy services and can provide an escort for visits to hospital or clinics.

4.5.2 Retirement village development costs

The costs of developing a retirement village are considerable. For example, in 2007 the cost of constructing a village with 12,000 square metres of buildings on a site that has a total size of two hectares (five acres) was approximately £1,400 per square metre. This equated to an initial investment of roughly £25 million. Another recently introduced financial model that has been applied to retirement villages is the private finance initiative (PFI). Under these schemes a capital project is designed, built, financed and managed by a private sector consortium, under a contract that typically lasts for 30 years. The private consortium will be regularly paid from public money depending on its performance throughout that period. One advantage of this model for local authorities is that they can engage in major developments such as retirement villages without having to commit to large capital outlays. However, some critics claim that, as with any form of hire purchase, buying a product over a longer period of time is ultimately more expensive. It has, however, become a popular option. For example, in 2008 Cheshire County Council announced plans to build five retirement villages as part of a PFI.

Once a village is built there are two main models for generating income from residents: ownership and mixed tenure. In an ownership model, property is all owner-occupied and care is funded via a range of financial arrangements, varying in their detail according to local circumstances and the availability of funding. Mixed tenure offers a range of options, usually a combination of outright ownership, shared ownership and rental. This is often part of an aim to ensure a mixed community and offer choices to those with a property to sell. Shared ownership usually falls within the definition of 'affordable housing'. Most housing association and charitable providers, as well as the private sector, deliberately seek to attract a proportion of residents who pay for their own care for a variety of reasons, including risk management and community balance. Not-for-profit organisations often operate a mixed tenure model, while private developers are more likely to choose 100% ownership. This is partly because it is easier for not-for-profit organisations to attract government subsidies for housing with care developments; private developers have to rely on a purely business model. Managing mixed tenure can be challenging, largely because of the potentially complex relationships between residents, developers, managers and care providers. Additional complexities exist in terms of funding arrangements, including shared equity schemes and eligibility for benefits such as housing benefit and income support. The reasons for considering mixed tenure are comprehensively described in a Housing LIN factsheet (King and Mills, 2005). These include: increased demand as a result of the rise in older owner-occupiers seeking specialist accommodation; encouragement from the government as part of housing policy that promotes tenure diversification; and making social-rented housing affordable by using receipts from sales to reduce borrowing. Mixed-tenure schemes vary in terms of whether different tenures are integrated or segregated. The implications of this for social interaction and the development of a sense of community are explored in Chapter Seven.

4.5.3 The development of retirement villages in the UK

Retirement villages have been slow to take off in the UK compared with the US, but they are now the fastest growing area of the upper end of the residential property market. This is largely because today's older generation have more disposable income than any previous one, and they aspire to live longer, stay healthier and do more in later life than previous generations. Many of this generation are 'downsizing' at an earlier age, which means that the average age of purchasers is decreasing. In addition, an increasing number of people in their 40s and 50s want to trade down from a large detached property to a community that they see as secure and private.

So far the retirement villages that have been built in the UK are considerably smaller than those in the US, largely due to stringent planning regulations and a lack of space, but there is a definite trend towards increased size. The main drivers for the rapid spread of retirement villages are the same as those for extra care housing: the ageing population, the popularity of the concept of ageing in place, the development of new lifestyles in older life and a general recognition of the need for greater choice and flexibility in housing options for older people (Heywood et al, 2001).

Retirement villages first appeared in the UK in the 1950s as groups of privately owned residences for retired older people in relatively good health who were able to live independently. However, they have diversified to include purpose-built CCRCs. These usually incorporate a range of facilities and social and recreational activities, and some villages now make provision for a broader age range, including people who are still in employment. Flexible care is typically available, including home help, personal care, health care, home maintenance, eating facilities and transport. In marketing terms, retirement communities use images of positive lifestyles for older people that incorporate concepts such as successful ageing and active retirement. They also claim to offer opportunities for companionship, privacy, and a relatively worry-free environment.

An example comes from Denham Garden village in Buckinghamshire, which has recently been expanded to provide 326 cottages for people aged 55 or over. The village is marketed as a 'community of like-minded people' that offers a 'carefree, active existence in your later years'.

4.5.4 Living in a retirement village

To date there has been relatively little research that focuses on the experiences of people living in retirement villages in the UK. One of the few studies that has been carried out found a variety of interpretations of the concept of 'community' among the residents (Croucher et al, 2003). For most, it meant being good neighbours and having opportunities for social interaction. Although community was important for most residents, achieving a balance between community and privacy was crucial and the lack of pressure to participate in community activities was also valued. Another study of an English purpose-built retirement village reported that residents perceived such communities as a positive alternative to both nursing homes and reliance on family support (Biggs et al, 2001). However, while many residents moved in with the aim of making new friends and combating loneliness, frailty could be a major factor in social exclusion (Bernard et al, 2007). A review by Croucher et al (2006) explored the evidence from recent studies along with data from an ongoing comparative evaluation of seven retirement communities. The authors concluded that retirement villages have great potential to address a range of policy objectives, including promoting independence, choice and quality of life for older people. A systematic review by Blandy et al (2003) found overall high levels of resident satisfaction in gated villages, although a sense of community and neighbourliness were of little importance to residents.

One criticism of retirement villages is that they are only a realistic option for the well-off. Phillipson (2007) argued that there are 'significant inequalities' between those older people who are able to make decisions about where and with whom to live, and those who feel marginalised and alienated by changes in the communities in which they have 'aged in place'. People living in retirement villages presumably fall into the former category. Others have characterised retirement communities as being only for the old (Kuhn, 1977) and even as systems of social control (Turner, 2007). Criticism has also been levelled at gated retirement developments, which usually take the form of walled or fenced housing schemes to which public access is restricted, often protected by CCTV and/or security personnel, and usually characterised by legal agreements that tie the residents to a common code of conduct. Blakely and Snyder (1999) identified three broad types of gated community (GC): lifestyle GCs, where gates provide security for leisure activities and residences within; prestige GCs, which have little differentiation from ordinary residential areas but gates are used as a form of social distinction and symbol of prestige; and security zone GCs, where gates are motivated by fear of crime and outsiders. This form of housing has seen huge growth in South America, South Africa, the Middle East and Southeast Asia, although many communities of this type are not just for older people. In Europe, Canada, Australia and New Zealand the development of gated communities is not so widespread. One example is provided by Westbury Fields, a gated retirement village developed by the St Monica Trust in the southwest of England. This scheme is profiled in Case Study Eight below.

Case Study Eight: Westbury Fields retirement village, Bristol, England

Westbury Fields is a gated development situated in a residential part of Bristol, a large city in southwest England. It was one of the first mixed-tenure retirement villages in the UK, aiming to support a diverse population from different socio-economic backgrounds across a variety of housing tenures and care options, ranging from active, independent residents to those requiring a high degree of care and support. The village is home to over 200 older people, who occupy privately owned retirement apartments, a nursing care home and an extra care housing facility. The village is surrounded by a fence and both entrances have security gates and CCTV and the site staff includes 24-hour security personnel. A study of the village (Evans and Means, 2007) reported that some residents felt that the gated nature of the development made them feel safer, although they also concluded that the gating was likely to present a psychological and physical barrier to integration with people living in local communities.

Critics of gated schemes include the Royal Institute of Chartered Surveyors (RICS), who view them as enclaves for well-off city dwellers who want to shut themselves away in high-security compounds, with surveillance cameras, electronic gates and even private security guards. Their concern is that if allowed to develop unchecked, this trend will breed hostility and threaten the social cohesion of the UK's cities (Minton, 2006). There is some evidence that older residents feel safer in gated villages (Evans and Means, 2007), although it could be argued that this is more of a perception than a reality and that gating can actually attract criminal activity. These concerns have been shared by the UK charity Age Concern, whose director general, Gordon Lishman, said: 'The best are probably the villages which offer a variety of ownership and renting options and integrate with the wider community, as living in a gated development could lead to older people missing out on valuable contact with people of other age groups' (*Telegraph*, 21 November 2007).

Although gated villages may raise concerns about social inclusion, public policy is firmly in favour of retirement villages in general. In 2005 government minister Stephen Ladyman declared: 'We want more of these villages and need to see this part of the spectrum of choice for older people available to everyone in the country' (Community Care, 5 May 2005).[4] Government enthusiasm for this form of retirement accommodation is largely based on its desire to promote mixed communities. For example, the report of the Urban Task Force (Rogers, 1999) urged the creation of mixed-tenure neighbourhoods in order to reduce the physical and social barriers between income groups. These, it was felt, are symbolised by the distinctions between social-rented and owner-occupied areas of housing. In response to some of these concerns there is now a move towards mixed-tenure retirement villages, which combine privately owned retirement apartments with social housing. The extent to which such developments can succeed in creating 'balanced' communities is open to debate (Evans and Means, 2007). Similarly, a study by Cheshire (2007) concluded that ensuring a mix of income in residential settings generally does not necessarily lead to stronger, more sustainable communities, although they had often become pleasant places in which to live and work.

While retirement villages may have been slower to emerge in the UK than in some other countries, there are certainly signs of rapid growth now. For example the Extra Care Charitable Trust, one of the largest UK providers, had 32 villages in 2007 and planned to develop many more during the following 20 years. The average size of retirement villages is also increasing. For example, Lovat Fields village near Milton Keynes has 258 homes including 100 affordable rental homes, 90 affordable shared-ownership homes and 68 homes for private sale. This rapid expansion is largely driven by demand. Over 700 applications were received for the 258 properties available and the Milton Keynes Council Plan predicts that a further 9,286 people over the age of 60 will be living in the city by 2011. As a result of this level of demand a second village is now being planned in the area. Along with increased size comes a greater range of facilities, as described in the case studies in this chapter.

Private developers have largely targeted the luxury end of the retirement village market. For example, one company, which is an offshoot of North America's leading provider of 'gracious retirement living', is building a 'luxury retirement community for the elderly' on the site of a former hospital in Wales. This will incorporate 117 apartments with a waitress service dining room, beauticians and a range of recreation facilities. The company was quoted as saying 'This is a revolutionary concept in retirement living in the UK. It represents a wonderful way to enjoy a relaxing, safe and secure retired lifestyle, where the bills and maintenance are all taken care of. It is like being on holiday all the time' (icWales, 2007).

Despite this growing popularity, the development costs of retirement villages are extremely high and there are significant challenges, including obtaining the necessary planning permission. Most local authorities have little if any experience in dealing with planning applications of this kind. This has led to some confusion about how retirement villages should be treated in terms of land use. Schemes do of course differ from one another, but there has been much debate as to how retirement villages generally should be classified. The main issue is whether they should come into category C1 (hotels with no significant care), C2 (residential accommodation and care) or C3 (dwelling houses). These categories are important in relation to a range of associated planning issues. C3 development falls under normal housing policies within development plans and is subject to testing within the parameters of the overall housing requirements set by the development plan documents, whereas C2 falls under the same special housing policies as nursing homes and other residential institutions. Another planning consideration is whether or not to place a requirement to provide affordable housing. This requirement has significant financial implications, particularly for private developers who are more likely to operate purely commercial models without public subsidy. A range of other forms of 'planning gain' have also been added as requirements for approval. For example, permission for the development of Westbury Fields retirement village in southwest England included as a condition the improvement of nearby sports facilities and footpaths.

Another reason for the relatively slow rate of growth in retirement villages in the UK has been the difficulty of finding suitable land. As a result, two main types of site have commonly been used: rural sites that sit either on the edge of a town or in the middle of the countryside; and redevelopments of urban sites that involve change of use. Whiteley village, one of the first retirement villages in the UK, is an example of the former. It is an octagonal development of Grade II listed almshouse-style cottages, set in the 'tranquil and peaceful surroundings of 240 acres of woodland'.

One example of an urban site is a proposed development on land in the city of Exeter that was until recently part of a university campus. The campus has now been relocated and it is hoped to build a retirement village with 156 supported accommodation units and two nursing homes. This proposal is being supported by local residents, largely because it will provide a wide range of facilities that they can use in an area where many have recently closed down. These will include a restaurant, bank, coffee shop, library, a spa/gym, consulting facilities for visiting GPs and a day nursery for up to 25 children. This provides interesting opportunities for interaction between the village and the local population and highlights the different challenges that urban and rural villages face in terms of community engagement. This is explored in more detail in Chapter Six on the experience of community in housing with care settings.

Given these and other challenges, developers have become increasingly imaginative in their attempts to find suitable sites. Some recent examples include old hospitals, and even a former holiday camp. Typical indicators for a successful village are listed in Box 4.1.

Box 4.1: Criteria for a financially viable retirement village location
- more than one in five people over retirement age living in the locality;
- a level site, served by public transport, near shops, church and other facilities;
- available land of between three and five hectares;
- a high expected demand but low level of specialist provision;
- a site not more than five miles from a major centre of population;
- for mixed-tenure models, projected house prices of no less than half the cost of providing extra care dwellings, depending on the availability of subsidy;
- site-specific attractive features, for example a pleasant outlook, near a park, and/or absence of overriding unattractive features.

Many recent retirement village developments have been keen to adopt the Sustainable Communities agenda. For example, Green Park village in Reading has been conceived as a 'sustainable urban village', combining a retirement housing scheme with family homes, offices, shops, a primary school, a waterside park and a range of community facilities and open spaces.[5] The sustainable focus of this ambitious development includes the building of a new railway station, the use of locally sourced materials, minimum carbon emissions, renewable energy sources and wildlife corridors. There is some evidence that mixed land use of this type brings a range of potential benefits, including higher levels of walking and increased social cohesion (Sustainable Development Commission, 2006).

4.6 Conclusion

In this chapter I have suggested a range of reasons for the emergence of new forms of housing for older people, including increasing demand as a result of the ageing of the population and the unsuitability of much housing for older people. Retirement villages and extra care housing in particular have experienced rapid growth, largely because they have the potential to support government priorities for older people, including the promotion of independence in their own homes and opportunities for choice.

Both of these models of housing are evolving and they share many characteristics. They both typically offer a range of flexible housing and care options that can be tailored to individuals as their needs and preferences change, as well as providing 24-hour onsite care. The main difference between the two types comes in terms of scale, with retirement villages usually being considerably larger than extra care housing schemes, although the emergence of extra care 'villages' means that even this distinction is no longer so clear. Some retirement villages also incorporate a care home facility into which residents can move when their care needs reach a particular level. Crucially for the theme of this book, both forms of provision place great emphasis on the provision of opportunities for social interaction in a community setting.

I have also explored how the two models have developed in the UK. Extra care housing is fairly new and has emerged as a hybrid, based initially on sheltered housing. In many areas it is replacing some sheltered housing and care home provision, largely because it is seen as more modern and less institutional. This chapter has also described arrangements for providing and funding the different elements of housing and care, which have become increasingly complex and varied. Retirement villages, on the other hand, have been around in the UK since the 1950s but they have been slow to take off until recently, largely due to relatively low levels of demand, the cost of obtaining suitable land sites and difficulties in obtaining planning permission. While the government has provided considerable funding for extra care housing schemes, often in partnership with local authorities and registered social landlords or housing associations, many retirement villages have been built by private developers and targeted at the more luxury sector of the housing market. As a result, they often have a higher design specification and include a wider range of facilities, such as health spas, swimming pools and libraries. New models of retirement village provision are continuing to be developed. For example, some newer villages offer a 'hotel-style' living option, whereby residents have all of their housework done and can either eat their meals in the village restaurant or have them delivered to their apartment. The considerable cost of developing and managing retirement villages is of course reflected in property prices and service charges.

Critics of retirement villages have portrayed them as 'elderly ghettoes' that are only affordable for the well-off. Some recent schemes have countered this by offering a range of tenures within a single village, combining private apartments with social housing, affordable housing and rented properties. Research into retirement villages is in its infancy in the UK, but the little that has been carried out has reported high levels of satisfaction among residents. However, lower levels of satisfaction and social wellbeing have been reported by residents with health problems such as sensory impairment and limited mobility.

This chapter has described the main features of housing with care and how two of the most popular models, extra care housing and retirement villages, have developed in the UK. In Chapter Six I will consider the extent to which these settings function as communities, as is frequently claimed by the organisations that develop and manage them. Before that, Chapter Five explores similar forms of provision in other countries.

Notes

[1] www.eac.org.uk

[2] See www.jrht.org.uk/Hartfields for further details of this scheme.

[3] More details can be found at www.housingcare.org/eac-quality-of-info-mark. aspx

[4] www.communitycare.co.uk

[5] www.greenparkvillage.co.uk

FIVE

An international perspective on retirement villages

5.1 Introduction

The first retirement villages were probably established in European countries for Roman soldiers who were no longer in peak fighting form and would therefore have swelled the ranks of the unemployed if they returned home. Much later the idea was resurrected in Europe in the form of housing schemes, often with connections to religion, that aimed to provide shelter and care for the aged. The concept spread to the US in the early 1900s, where their numbers grew along with the size of the older population and by 2001 there were around 2,000 retirement villages in the US, where they have become an extremely popular housing choice for later life. It is estimated that up to 12% of the older US population live in purpose-built retirement communities and such developments now account for roughly 11% of all new housing (Webster, 2002). The biggest development of this kind has more than 75,000 residents. The recent rapid growth of retirement villages has been driven by the increasing number of people in middle- to higher-income brackets who are tending to retire at an earlier age. It is now not uncommon for individuals and couples as young as 50 years to be purchasing retirement accommodation for immediate occupation. This, combined with increased life expectancies, is leading to a shortage of retirement accommodation in some countries. For example, in South Africa some retirement villages have 30-year waiting lists, which has led to annual price increases of up to 20%.

This chapter explores the history of retirement villages in several countries, including the US, Australia and New Zealand. It looks at how they have evolved to cater for the demographics of the baby boomer generation and the changing aspirations of older people by creating a variety of 'niche' markets.

5.2 Retirement villages in North America

Sun City in Central Florida was the first large-scale purpose-built retirement village in the US. It opened in 1960 and grew rapidly, selling 2,000 homes in the first year, and now has 40,000 residents. By 1999 there were an estimated 2,100 retirement villages in the US, housing about 750,000 people with an average age of 78. The majority of them are run by not-for-profit organisations but private developers are increasingly recognising the commercial potential of this market sector.

The population trends behind the burgeoning growth of retirement villages in the US are compelling. People born in the years following the Second World War have formed a major population bulge moving through the generations and these 'baby boomers' are now starting to form the largest-ever group of retirees. It has been estimated that by the year 2030 there will be 22 million Americans aged over 65, and 1 million over the age of 100 by 2040. In addition, at least 6.4 million North Americans aged 65 or older need long-term care, it is estimated that at least half of the population who are over 85 will need help with activities of daily living (United Seniors Health Council, 2002).

The baby boomer group number nearly 80 million and they have now started trickling into retirement communities. Well over 50% of the boomers are older than 50 already, and by 2030 they will all be in the 66 to 84 age range, making up 20% of the total population. Besides being a large swath of the population, boomers are considerably better off financially than earlier generations of retirees and the vast majority are homeowners. While a generation or two ago most retirees could only expect to live for a relatively short period after retirement, the boomers' generation now have 25 years or more to fill and, in many cases, the wealth to enjoy those years in considerable luxury. This has led to new models of later-life living, in which words such as 'senior' and 'retirement' have gone, to be replaced with concepts such as 'active ageing' and 'luxury lifestyles'.

The US has by far the largest retirement communities. For example, Laguna Woods village in California is a four square mile (1,036-hectare) retirement community for 'active adults' that is home to 18,000 residents with an average age of 78. The sheer scale of this development is indicated by the fact that it has 94 different housing floor plans, employs a 100-person security team and raises over $67,000 a year in fines levied by its own traffic police force. Even larger is The Villages, a network of smaller neighbourhoods in Florida that is home to about 75,000 Americans. See Case Study Nine below for more details.

Case Study Nine: The Villages, Florida, US

The Villages:
- is the largest retirement community in the US;
- started as a trailer park of 400 homes in the 1960s;
- now covers 20,000 acres and is home to 75,000 people aged 55 and over in 38,000 houses, with plans to extend to 100,000 residents;
- in 2005 sold 4,263 new homes, bringing in over $1 billion;
- has a population that is 97% white;
- has its own TV channel, radio station, daily newspaper and monthly magazine;
- is designed as a golf-cart community, with over 100 miles of golf track;
- includes a wide range of leisure facilities, including 30 golf courses and a similar number of swimming pools;
- includes an imitation Spanish colonial town;

Each 'village' within the overall development has only one style/price band of housing, as a form of asset protection. They are not strictly villages because there is no mixed land use and commercial enterprises are restricted to separate zones or malls.

The US retirement community sector is extremely well established and a wide range of models have developed. A property locator service called Retirenet[1] lists ten main categories based on the needs and interests of residents, as shown in Table 5.1.

Table 5.1: Ten categories of US retirement villages

Category	Characteristics
Active lifestyles	This category encompasses the entire range of independent retirement living. These communities are designed to promote a rich life experience based on active recreation and social interaction with other seniors
Golf communities	Golf communities are centred around courses ranging from 9-hole up to 18-hole championship courses
Upscale community living	Premier upscale homes and communities. Homes in this category typically range from $500,000 to several million dollars
Manufactured home	Manufactured and modular homes aim to provide affordable housing with similar amenities as site-built homes
Recreational vehicle	Aimed at older people who are motor home enthusiasts
Rental	Provide the same homes and amenities as other communities, but offer short-term, seasonal, and annual rentals as well
General care	Communities and facilities encompassing a category of general care
Continuing care	Communities found in this category offer facilities and amenities ranging from active lifestyles to skilled nursing care
Assisted living	Assisted living communities feature facilities and staff that offer residents an extra level of assistance in their everyday lives
Skilled nursing	Skilled nursing communities exist to care for seniors who are no longer able to care for themselves

Source: Adapted from Retirenet; www.retirenet.com

This variety of specialist provision reflects the way in which retirement villages have adapted to meet their increasing popularity across a range of socio-economic backgrounds and levels of care need. This diversity is also reflected in the range of prices, which start at around $65,000 in the manufactured home category and go up to several million dollars for upscale community living.

In these new-style housing complexes older people are offered the opportunity to try out daring new pursuits, such as skydiving or white water rafting. Many older people are also choosing to continue working, at least part time, while others split their time between two residences. Some land developers are targeting these lifestyles by including specific facilities in their retirement villages, such as good access to airports and high-speed internet. One company even donated 4,000 acres (1,600 hectares) of land to a new international airport near Panama City in Florida, which it hopes will serve both locals and retirees who move into its developments in the area.

There is now a burgeoning market for luxury retirement villages, both in the US and elsewhere. One recent example is Santa Marta in Kansas. This $45 million development provides accommodation across 138 independent-living apartments, 24 independent-living villas, 32 assisted-living apartments, 16 memory-support units and 32 nursing beds. Amenities include a dining room, cafe, aquatic centre, fitness centre, arts and crafts studio, card room, games room, bar, business centre, library, salon, chapel and heated underground parking. Such amenities come with a price tag to match, with entrance fees starting at $185,000 plus monthly service fees. Another recent example of a retirement village aimed firmly at the 'well heeled' is the Stratford in Colorado, which, according to an article in the *Denver Post*, aims to provide the 'elegance, pampering and services of a luxurious five-star hotel' within a development of independent-living apartments and an assisted-living centre.[2] Plans for this kind of scheme are based on estimates that between 8% and 12% of older people in the US can afford this kind of luxury retirement accommodation.

There are a range of financial models for providing housing and care within US retirement villages. It is usual to charge an entrance fee plus a monthly fee, but the size of the fees and what they cover varies considerably. Three models are particularly common: life contracts, which cover unlimited long-term nursing care within the monthly fee; sliding contracts, which include a limited duration of long-term nursing care, beyond which fees rise as care needs increase; and fee-for-service contracts, in which residents pay a reduced monthly fee but pay full daily rates for long-term nursing care. Variations of these basic models can also be found. To complicate things further, all or part of the entrance fee can be refunded, or it might be refundable for a period of time before becoming non-refundable. Purchasing retirement accommodation can cost from $20,000 to more than $100,000, and there are also monthly fees to pay, which can range from $1,000 to $4,000, depending on care needs (Helpguide, 2008). Many villages offer a flexible system whereby residents can buy care packages as their needs change. Health care services may be provided in facilities that are on site or in the wider community.

Retirement villages are widely perceived to bring a number of benefits to existing communities, including job creation and a boost to the local economy. However, they can also lead to local concerns. For example, when Peninsula United Methodist Homes applied for permission to build a 346-unit CCRC in the town of Ocean View, Maryland, US, the town council was worried about a range of issues, including setting a precedent for building density, the potential impact on local services and the fact that the new residents might outweigh the existing 526 registered voters in local elections. In his entertaining and informative book *Leisureville*, Andrew Blechman (2008) outlines some of the potential effects of large-scale retirement villages on local government structures and the provision of resources, both natural and human made. For example, people living in The Villages, home to over 75,000 older people in Florida, outnumber the county residents by a considerable margin and have succeeded in changing the basis on which local representatives are elected. The potential impact of large retirement developments on the areas in which they sit can be considerable in many ways. For example, the developer of The Villages is one of Florida's top Republican donors and many political candidates often visit the development as part of their campaigns in order to court the potential 75,000 votes. This is not surprising when you consider that residents are some of the most reliable voters in the state, with a turnout rate of nearly 80%.

However, most counties remain keen to attract retirement villages, largely due to the assumption that the extra tax income generated will outweigh the cost of extra services that have to be provided. This is borne out by a study carried out at the University of Cincinnati of a proposed 69-acre (28-hectare) retirement development. This concluded that, although the village would have an impact on the local fire and police departments, this would be outweighed by the tax revenue of $600,000. This desire to welcome retirement communities is reflected in the fact that many states have allowed developers to create independent districts that are exempt from a range of restrictions, including land use laws.

In the US a distinction is often made between naturally occurring retirement communities (NORCs) and formally organised retirement communities. The former are neighbourhoods that have evolved into a community of older people because the younger people have migrated away and those remaining have aged in place. They are not generally made up of purpose-built housing for older people, nor are they specifically designed to meet their health and social care needs. However, they are sometimes seen as providing the opportunity to deliver targeted services in a cost-effective way. This has led to the development of a national NORCs initiative by the US Administration on Aging, as well as a range of projects encouraging activities and community involvement among NORC residents.

About 80 communities across the US are experimenting with programmes in 25 states to support about 25,000 people aged 60 or over who want to remain in their neighbourhoods. These initiatives are funded through public–private partnerships and usually charge nominal membership and activities fees. For example, one programme, called Senior Friendly Neighborhoods in Upper Park Heights, northwest Baltimore, supports 950 people with an average age of 80 who live in 11 apartment buildings. Funding comes from a range of sources, including a federal grant, the city of Baltimore and a philanthropic foundation. A range of activities are provided, including trips to concerts, local workshops, a free shopping bus and a regular onsite health clinic. Another example, Beacon Hill village in Boston, demonstrates the aim of these programmes to provide a supportive environment for older people while enabling them to remain connected with the communities in which they grew up, as opposed to moving to purpose-built retirement developments. The 500 members pay an annual fee of $600 for an individual or $850 for a household in return for a range of services, including grocery shopping, home maintenance and cultural events. It also refers residents in need of home health care to a service provider that it has vetted and with which it has negotiated discounts. The scheme has an annual budget of almost $0.5 million, almost half of which comes from donors and foundations, which allows it to employ the full-time equivalent of five people and to offer some subsidised memberships. The model has been developed further in California, where an initiative called Avenidas Vvillage is trying to cover a much larger area in the form of 10 entire towns.

Evaluation of such initiatives suggests a range of potential benefits for residents. For example, in a survey of 500 NORC residents sampled from each of the 24 longest-running federal demonstration programmes, the vast majority of respondents reported that they knew and spoke to more people than they used to and that they participated in more group activities and events and left the confines of their home more often. They also tended to feel healthier than they had prior to participation in the NORC sites.

With a huge number of baby boomers moving towards retirement, developers are increasingly looking for new niches in the market, including what are known as 'affinity communities' for people with specific interests. These include schemes for faith-based groups, such as the Apostolic retirement village, a Christian not-for-profit community in Kansas. Another relatively new development is gay and lesbian retirement communities, such as Rainbow Vision (see Case Study Ten). There are an estimated 3 million gay and lesbian seniors currently living in the United States. Figures from the National Gay and Lesbian Task Force indicate that this number is expected to more than double over the next 25 years as the 'gayby boomer' generation moves into retirement. Because many gay older people find traditional retirement communities unprepared or unwilling to meet the needs of gay, lesbian, bisexual and transgender (GLBT) residents, the demand for gay retirement communities is growing. Although this has been identified as a potentially lucrative market for retirement villages, based on the premise that many gays want to spend their retirement years in places where they are comfortable being themselves, relatively few have opened so far. This is largely because of a range of challenges, including raising the funding and finding a location that is gay friendly. Anti-discrimination laws prevent villages from marketing themselves as exclusively for gay older people, but they do promote themselves as gay friendly. However, very few villages of this nature have been built and some are finding it difficult to sell properties.

Case Study Ten: Rainbow Vision, Santa Fe, California, US

This retirement village provides 146 units spread out over 13 acres (5 hectares), costing from $250,000 to $310,000 each. This village was initially promoted almost exclusively to the gay community through images of same-sex couples. However, slow sales led the developers to attempt to broaden the appeal by advertising to mixed-gender couples and offering non-residents the use of facilities. This led to concern among residents who, although not seeking an all-gay enclave, were keen to live in an environment with a majority of gay men and women.

Green retirement villages are another recent niche development in the US, aimed at the 'Woodstock' generation, who grew up with the environmental movement of the 1960s and 1970s. One example is Victoria Gardens in Florida, which advertises homes as having a carbon footprint that is 20% to 30% less than that of a 'typical household'. Environmentally friendly features include solar attic fans, green-fibre recycled insulation, motion-sensor triggered lighting, energy-efficient windows and appliances, and garages fitted with electric-vehicle charging stations. The developers are confident that the baby boomer generation of retirees will consider paying a premium for environmentally friendly features such as these and they plan to build 20,000 of these homes over the next 10 years.

Another recent development is the building of university-based retirement communities (UBRCs). Although still at a fairly experimental stage, there are about 60 university-linked retirement communities already built and many more planned. They are aimed at older people who want learning to be a large part of their lifestyle and allow for residents to access university classes, cultural events and facilities. For the universities they provide an opportunity to bolster their revenues through sales, rentals and potentially increased donations by retired staff. There are a number of different UBRC models, but many specifically target older people with links to the academic institution. For example, Oak Hammond retirement village opened in 2004 close to the University of Florida. About 12% of the residents are retired university staff and 50% are alumni.

The US boom in retirement villages looks set to continue around a range of new models. For example, one developer, Erickson, plan to add 50 new communities over the next decade, representing an investment of $12 billion by 2017. However, some commentators have expressed doubts as to the sustainability of the large retirement village model, particularly in the light of economic slowdown, and have raised the spectre of older people becoming isolated in half-empty developments. It is certainly true that the slowing of the housing market in 2008/09 had an impact on sales of retirement housing, largely because people wanting to move into new schemes were finding it difficult to sell their existing properties. Some developers responded to this by introducing innovative initiatives, such as the Why Wait? programme launched by Senior Living Communities in the US. This enabled prospective residents to purchase at a greatly reduced initial price, of up to 25% of the full value, and pay the remaining 75% at a later date when their own home had sold.

Another challenge to continued growth in this sector is the availability of land that is suitable for ever-larger retirement villages. In some cases, increasing land and development costs are being passed on to residents, many of whom are struggling to meet them. For example, in 2007 the residents of Touchmark 'resort-style' community in Alberta, Canada, suddenly found that their service charge was being increased by up to 100%. This was seen as a disaster by many residents, for whom it meant that their financial plans were severely disrupted. In some cases their ability to remain in the community where they had intended to spend the rest of their lives was in doubt.

5.3 Retirement villages in Australia and New Zealand

The retirement village sector is also well established in Australia, and recent growth has been rapid. In 1996 there were 520 retirement villages in Australia, housing about 56,500 people, or 2.7% of the population aged 65 years or over. By 2006 the number of villages had increased to over 1,500, with about 140,000 residents, representing about 5% of those aged 65 or over. In certain areas such as the Gold Coast, the figure is as high as 12%. It has been predicted that there will be 2,900 villages by 2016 and 4,300 by 2026. These large numbers translate into big business. The industry in Australia is currently worth about AU$74 billion, with developers making substantial profits in management fees, on top of the margin made each time a property changes hands. A new kind of development is planned on the Australian Gold Coast in the form of a vertical retirement village. This luxury retirement complex will comprise 350 apartments in three eight-storey buildings, along with a cinema, a gymnasium, a swimming pool and extensive office space.

One distinction between Australian and US retirement villages is the financial model. While most North American residents rent or purchase their retirement units, a deferred-fee model is prevalent in Australia. Under this arrangement a management fee is paid on leaving the village, usually somewhere between 2.5% and 10% of the purchase price of a retirement unit for each year spent in the village. However, despite the attraction of a low upfront financial outlay, there has been considerable suspicion of this model and the unpredictability of the overall costs. As a result, there has been a recent move towards introducing a more transparent pricing structure.

Specialist models of retirement village are beginning to emerge in Australia, although not on the same scale as in the US. For example, plans have recently been announced for the first Australian GLBT retirement village near Daylesford, which has one of the largest homosexual populations in rural Australia.

As in many other countries, the recent growth of the retirement village sector in New Zealand has been driven by demographics. In 2007, 11.5% of the population were over 65, a figure that is expected to rise to 19% by 2025 and 25% by 2050 (Ministry of Social Development, 2001). Recent estimates suggest that 25,000 people, 5% of the population aged 65 and over, live in about 400 retirement villages (Grant, 2006). These are predominantly new-build developments, occupied by people who are aged 70 and over and largely widowed. A considerable degree of regulation has been introduced in New Zealand through the 2003 Retirement Villages Act, which sets out a legal framework for operators to run villages and requires them to register with the registrar of retirement villages, while also providing protection for residents. In addition, in 2008 a Retirement Villages Code of Practice was introduced. This sets minimum standards that all villages must meet by 2009.

5.4 Retirement villages and other housing with care models in the rest of the world

The retirement village industry has also started to emerge in many other countries around the world in recent years, although it is still far behind that in the US, Australia and New Zealand. Chapter Four explored how this form of housing for later life is now starting to become popular in the UK. In Spain, for example, retirement villages for English-speaking people are starting to spring up on the Costa del Sol and the Costa Blanca. Other countries where retirement villages are now being seen include Germany, Italy and the Philippines. Retirement villages are even becoming a popular option in countries where great importance is traditionally placed on extended family support. For example, several developments of this type have already been built in India and it has been estimated that up to 1 million of the population of 80 million older people could be attracted to this type of accommodation.

Mexico is another less-developed country where retirement villages are starting to appear, although the difference here is that they are aimed at North American retirees, attracted by the fact that the cost of living is 30% cheaper than in the US. One example is Paradise Cove near Sonora, which is only an hour's drive from Mexico's border with Arizona and near to the site of a new international airport. This retirement village is closely based on the US model, offering extensive leisure facilities including several golf courses. It is thought that 100,000 North American retirees live in Mexico already and it is suggested that, with 76 million American baby boomers hitting retirement age over the next two decades, up to 8 million may choose to move there in the future.

In some countries other models of retirement living have become popular instead of villages and extra care housing. One such model is co-housing, whereby people choose the land, the design features and who to live with. Residents own their individual properties but share some communal facilities. The first co-housing was developed in Denmark in the 1970s, most of it being multigenerational to start with. The age-targeted co-housing model became increasingly popular and there are now over 200 completed co-housing communities for older people in Denmark. The model took off in the US in the late 1980s and over 5,000 Americans now live in about 75 co-housing communities. Many of them meet the environmentally sustainable housing agenda of today's baby boomer generation.

In Holland and some Scandinavian countries there has been a growing emphasis on integration and normalisation. For example, Ros Anders Gard in Sweden aims to create an intimate care setting through the provision of accommodation for 40 residents in four decentralised clusters of 10 units each. Fixtures and fittings are designed to produce a domestic rather than an institutional feel, including the use of house-style kitchens, in which the residents are encouraged to help with food preparation. There is also a trend towards multigenerational housing that includes older people. One such scheme, Gyngemosegard in Denmark, combines three-bedroom family apartments and one-bedroom units and co-housing for older people. Promoting social interaction between younger and older people is seen as a priority. In the Netherlands one popular model of continuing care is known as 'Apartment for Life'. This concept has many similarities with extra care housing, with an emphasis on promoting independence through flexible care packages. The care here, however, is rigorously separated from the housing and is purchased from several providers, according to residents' needs. The importance of social networks is recognised and maintained by encouraging the involvement of families, friends and volunteers. A recent development is the aim to deliver hospital-type interventions in this setting, including minor operations and support for psychiatric patients. The vision is that in future people will only have to leave their apartment if they require treatments that necessitate intensive care beds. Innovative models of housing with care are also found in Finland, where the Metsatahti scheme in Helsinki combines housing for older people with a day-care centre for infants. Many of the communal spaces are shared, including the kitchen and dining room, and provide a venue for a range of intergenerational activities. Here again the emphasis is on small, familiar units, with older residents living in groups of four or five. More details of these and several other pioneering forms of provision can be found in *Design for assisted living* (Regnier, 2002).

5.5 Conclusion

In this chapter I have presented a broad picture of how retirement villages have developed around the world. The focus has been on their increasing popularity, largely as a result of ageing populations and changes in lifestyle aspirations. As previously discussed, the US has witnessed the greatest growth by far in this sector, in terms of both the size and number of its retirement villages. It is estimated that almost 12% of the older population live in purpose-built retirement settings, the largest of which has over 75,000 residents. Another interesting feature of retirement villages in the US is their focus on golf and other leisure activities. This is in contrast to the UK sector, where the provision of care is far more central to the way in which retirement villages are targeted at and marketed to older people. The US is also unique in the way that a range of niche markets have developed, including retirement villages for people from GLBT groups, the green movement, religious organisations and university alumni. Retirement villages are also well established as a popular choice in Australia, New Zealand and South Africa, while they are developing rapidly in several other countries including Italy, Germany, Spain and India. In some European countries different models of retirement housing have become popular, such as co-housing and small, domestic-style types of accommodation. These are based on a very different philosophy from retirement villages, particularly in terms of their focus on intergenerational social interaction.

This chapter has explored the main features of extra care housing and retirement villages in the UK and around the world. The next chapter provides an assessment of the extent to which these settings live up to their ambitions to function as communities for older people.

Notes

[1] www.retirenet.com

[2] www.denverpost.com/headlines/ci_10340071

SIX

Promoting a sense of community in housing with care settings

6.1 Introduction

Some forms of housing with care, particularly extra care housing and retirement villages, are marketed as communities for older people who have similar interests and lifestyles. This kind of marketing aims to appeal to older people's aspirations for community living and the fact that many feel alienated from a youth-focused society that sees ageing as a burden and places little value on the contribution that older people can make to society. There is no doubt that such settings are becoming increasingly popular and the evidence suggests that a sense of community is one of the main factors in choosing retirement housing. Given this, it is important to consider how the development of a sense of community can be promoted in housing with care schemes. This chapter explores the experiences of residents in terms of opportunities for social interaction and identifies a range of factors that can affect the development of a sense of community belonging.

6.2 How extra care housing and retirement villages market themselves as communities

Housing with care schemes are increasingly being marketed as communities. This is particularly evident from the descriptions found on many retirement village websites. For example, at Roseland Parc in Cornwall, 'The village community atmosphere will allow you to forge new friendships with like-minded people who share your interests, your joys and your challenges in life'.[1] Similarly, Richmond village in Coventry offers 'peace, security and above all a real sense of community and gives residents genuine peace of mind'.[2] What is striking about much of this marketing material is that the emphasis is on similarity rather than diversity. The use of the term 'village' is also interesting, given that many of these developments do not appear to fit with common usage of the word. For example, examination of a guide to 76 schemes that are described by their developers or managers as retirement villages (EAC, 2008b) reveals that many are in fact single buildings containing as few as 29 individual flats. As shown in Chapters Four and Five, there are also many larger schemes that appear on the surface to be much more village-like, comprising numerous buildings and a range of facilities. However, even these are generally much smaller in size than most definitions of a village. As quoted by Bernard (2008) Ordnance Survey considers a village to be a centre of population with an area of less than 2.5 square kilometres and always having a church, while the Department of Transport's criteria include a minimum of 20 houses and at least 600 metres of frontage. It seems clear that 'village' is widely used as a descriptor by retirement housing developers because it helps to create the image of a close-knit and harmonious community that many of us associate with village life, however imaginary and idealistic such perceptions might actually be. This level of focus on community has been less evident in relation to extra care housing, largely because it is usually developed as a form of social provision rather than as a commercial enterprise. Even so, social landlords and other stakeholders are keen to highlight the opportunities for community living that extra care housing provides. For example, Sandwell Metropolitan Borough Council describes the 'vibrant and stimulating community atmosphere' that can be found in extra care housing (Sandwell Borough Council, 2008). This focus on 'community' is largely a reflection of what is perceived to be important to people who are making decisions about retirement housing.

6.3 Defining a sense of community

Chapter Two provides a detailed discussion of the challenge of defining 'community' and the continued relevance of the concept to individuals and governments. To summarise, most theories of community have focused on three key elements: place attachment, shared interests and a sense of common identity. For many people social interaction is at the heart of a sense of community, as reflected in the concepts of social networks and social capital. Much recent literature has argued that geographical place is becoming less important as a factor in a sense of community, largely because social networks are far more diverse than they used to be. It has also been suggested that shared interests and identities are increasingly important factors in a sense of community. For example, religious belief, ethnic background and leisure pursuits have all been identified as more important than place as defining characteristics of community. In the UK, the promotion of 'community' has been central to numerous initiatives launched by recent Labour governments, based on the premise that communities are by their very nature a force for social cohesion. This assumption has been widely challenged on the grounds that communities can also be oppressive and conformist, and often include considerable amounts of conflict (e.g. Taylor, 2003). There has been a recent resurgence in interest about place attachment, particularly among environmental psychologists, and its role in establishing and maintaining a sense of identity across the lifecourse.

In this book I have highlighted the importance of local neighbourhood as a venue for everyday social interactions that are central to the development and maintenance of a sense of community. This emphasis on the role of the built environment in community is particularly appropriate to housing with care developments such as extra care housing and retirement villages. These are characterised by well-defined physical boundaries, and a range of design features are included specifically to support the development of a sense of community. This chapter explores residents' views and experiences of living in retirement housing. It then goes on to consider the extent to which these developments can promote a sense of community and to discuss some specific features that may contribute towards this.

6.4 Residents' views and experiences of community

Despite widespread portrayals of contemporary societies that suffer from a decline in community, there is evidence that it is a concept that is alive and flourishing and still of considerable importance to the majority of people. In a recent survey of 1,000 adults (Marsh, 2006) the majority of respondents felt that neighbourliness had not changed during the past five years and about 20% thought that it had actually improved. This figure was highest for people aged 65 or over, at 27%. A majority also felt that there was a sense of community and that community remained an important aspect of everyday life. Good relations were seen by 60% as a way of reducing stress and feeling happier and healthier as well as being important to a sense of safety and security.

Are such views shared by older people living in extra care housing and retirement villages? The research evidence for the experiences of people living in such developments in the UK is small but growing. A study of one of the first continuing care retirement villages in England found various interpretations of the concept of 'community' among residents (Croucher et al, 2003). For many it meant being good neighbours and having opportunities for social interaction. Community was undoubtedly important for most residents, but achieving a balance between community and privacy was also crucial, including a desire not to feel pressurised to participate in community activities. A study by Biggs et al (2001) of a purpose-built retirement village reported that residents perceived such communities as a positive alternative to both nursing homes and reliance on family support. Many residents had moved into the village with the aim of making new friends and combating loneliness, although frailty tended to increase the risk of social exclusion (Bernard et al, 2007).

More recently, a review of housing with care for later life (Croucher et al, 2006) explored the evidence from a range of studies alongside data from an ongoing comparative evaluation of seven retirement housing schemes. They concluded that retirement villages have great potential to address a range of policy objectives, including promoting independence, choice and quality of life for older people. A systematic review by Blandy et al (2003) found high overall levels of resident satisfaction, although in this study a sense of community and neighbourliness were a relatively low priority for residents. In their study of a mixed-tenure retirement village in southwest England, Evans and Means (2007) found contrasting views among residents on the extent to which the village functioned as a community. For example one care home resident described it as 'a real community of very diverse people to mix with' (p 23), while someone living in the extra care housing part of the village commented: 'I don't really regard myself as being part of a community, simply because I don't know any of the other people here' (p 42). There was also recognition that, as in any community, not everyone will become friends. Several residents reported that they found it difficult to develop friendships. Others were clear that they were not looking for friendship and were happy with their own company. The authors concluded that those residents who did feel part of a community tended to identify with the area of the village in which they lived rather than with the village as a whole. A more detailed description of the mixed-tenure model used in this scheme and its impact on a sense of community can be found in Chapter Seven.

Evans and Vallelly (2007) interviewed residents in six extra care housing schemes as part of their study into social wellbeing. Overall, residents reported high levels of satisfaction with their quality of life and said that friends within the scheme and contacts with the wider community were important factors. A number of other studies provide evidence for the importance of social interaction and social networks in promoting quality of life in long-term care settings (for example, Phillipson, 1997; Godfrey et al, 2004). Evans and Vallelly reported that a minority of residents were less integrated socially and felt isolated or lonely, particularly those with physical or cognitive impairments. This supports earlier findings (Percival, 2001; Croucher et al, 2006) and will be discussed further in Chapter Seven in terms of the challenge of promoting diversity in retirement housing.

6.5 The role of social interaction in promoting quality of life and a sense of community

As discussed in Chapter Two, one of the strongest themes to emerge from the large body of theoretical writing about community is the role and importance of social interaction. This can be seen in the emphasis that Tönnies and Loomis (1957) placed on different kinds of social relations and the concerns that Durkheim (1964) voiced about what he viewed as the breakdown of community values. More recently, the work of Putnam (2000) has been particularly influential, with his focus on social capital as the core feature of community identity. However, there is a considerable body of evidence to indicate the broader role of social interaction in promoting wellbeing in a range of settings. For example, social engagement has been linked to higher wellbeing among hospital patients (Gilbart and Hirdes, 2000), while having a greater number of social contacts has been associated with lower rates of depressive symptoms (Sugisawa et al, 2002). Some research literature even goes as far as suggesting that higher levels of social engagement are associated with lower mortality rates (Flacker and Kiely, 2003) and decreased risk of dementia (Sugisawa et al, 2002).

In their review of the literature on social wellbeing, Evans and Vallelly (2007) identified widespread consensus on the importance of social networks and social interaction to quality of life and psychological and social wellbeing. They also explored the possible links between social interaction and wellbeing. In addition, by contributing to a sense of purpose and attachment, social interaction can ameliorate the negative impact of past events and experiences. For Godfrey et al (2004), social relationships were the essence of 'ageing well' because they meet older people's needs for intimacy, comfort, support, companionship and fun, while Berkman et al (2000) concluded that social engagement can provide older people with a meaningful social role and thereby promotes a sense of purpose and attachment.

Some writers have distinguished between different types of relationships and their impact on wellbeing. A Japanese study found that relationships with friends were related to life satisfaction for older people living in the wider community, whereas relationships with family were more important for those living in residential care (Ho et al, 2003). A study of older people living in the community in Canada concluded that the quality of social relationships was more important to wellbeing than the quantity (Fox and Gooding, 1998). A more specific literature on housing with care examines different types of social interaction and concludes that there are more non-intimate relationships than intimate ones. However, it is the intimate relationships that are most important in terms of sense of wellbeing and, crucially, many of these are with family and friends from outside the housing setting (Potts, 1997). Similarly, *My home life* (Owen, 2006), a report into quality of life in care homes, reported that activities that connect residents to the outside community were highly valued.

In previous work (Evans and Means, 2007), retirement village residents suggested that social interaction was the most important factor in the development of a sense of community. Also relevant is a study of neighbourhood identity, based on three housing estates in Scotland (Robertson et al, 2008), which found that while established friendships were key factors in the development of social identity and belonging, everyday fleeting interactions were equally important. In our study of extra care housing (Evans and Vallelly, 2007), we found that a majority of tenants had opportunities for an active social life and for most tenants the friendships and acquaintances that they developed within their housing scheme provided the focus of their social lives. For others, maintaining social networks in the wider community was equally important.

There is mixed evidence regarding levels of social interaction in residential care settings compared with those for older people generally, but overall it seems that people in such settings who are physically frail and/or cognitively impaired have lower levels of social interaction than other residents. There also appear to be gender differences in levels of social interaction among older people. The Health Survey for England (Department of Health, 2002) found that men were more likely than women to perceive themselves as having a severe lack of social support and this self-perception was also more common in care homes than in private households. Men who had been resident in a care home for more than a year were more likely to have a severe lack of social support than those who had been resident for less time, while no such association was seen for women. This has implications for all housing with care settings, where men are usually in a minority due to differences in life expectancy. Evans and Vallelly (2007) found men to be at greater risk of social isolation in extra care housing schemes and identified the need to provide specific activities to match their interests and preferences.

The importance of connections and networks in the wider community outside housing with care settings is a recurring theme in the literature. The review by Croucher et al (2006) suggested that while such environments can be conducive to friendship for many residents, they can be alienating for those who are most vulnerable, including the cognitively impaired (Stacey-Konnert and Pynoos, 1992) and people with mobility problems (Bernard et al, 2004).

If the importance of social interaction to both the development of a sense of community and to general wellbeing is accepted – and the evidence is convincing – the next step is to explore what it is about environments in general, and particularly those that are commonly found in housing with care settings, that can influence the ways in which people interact. Factors will be discussed under five headings:

- The importance of the built environment
- Outdoor spaces
- Services and facilities
- Social activities
- Integration with the wider community.

6.6 The importance of the built environment

The design of the 'built environment', the indoor and outdoor spaces in which we live our lives, is important to all of us. However, it has added relevance for people living in housing with care settings because they are likely to spend considerable amounts of time within the housing scheme. They may also rely on their immediate environment to compensate for their physical or cognitive impairments. The importance of design in housing with care settings has been shown by a number of recent studies (for example, Vallelly et al, 2006; Evans and Means, 2007; Evans and Vallelly, 2007). Retirement villages and extra care housing are mostly purpose-built developments or recent conversions of older buildings, and are therefore usually compliant with good practice in terms of accessible design. This often includes features such as wide doorways for wheelchair users, the use of ramps and wheelchair-friendly bathrooms. One common feature of this type of housing with care is the indoor street or mall that runs through the centre of the scheme and around which most of the services and facilities are located. This provides a safe, dry and level environment that supports social interaction among residents, including those with impaired mobility. This is particularly important in the light of research evidence suggesting that casual social encounters are at least as important as formal social activities in terms of promoting a sense of community (Robertson et al, 2008). Photo 2 shows how the imaginative use of indoor spaces can provide venues for social interaction, in this case in the form of a snooker table.

Photo 2: Residents at Monica Wills House in Bristol play snooker in a communal space (Photograph by Zed Photography)

The research literature suggests that people who are physically frail and those with cognitive impairments tend to have lower levels of social interaction (Gilbart and Hirdes, 2000). Evans and Vallelly (2007) confirmed this finding in the extra care housing setting and concluded that, through its design, extra care can be an extremely supportive environment for social interaction among people who are physically frail. *Opening doors to independence* (Vallelly et al, 2006), a study of people with dementia living in extra care housing, concluded that appropriate design is crucial in enabling people with dementia to find their way around retirement housing schemes and to benefit from the opportunities to interact socially. They identified a range of design features that are commonly employed for this reason, but also noted that the evidence base to support these is extremely limited. However, the authors support a 'commonsense' approach that includes the use of appropriate signage, architectural landmarks, colour coding and incorporating small, familiar environments. Vallelly et al (2006) also explored two very different models for supporting people with dementia in extra care housing: integration with other residents and segregation into a separate unit, and examined which is most likely to encourage social interaction. Oak House, one example of the segregated model, is described in Case Study Eleven. Although they suggested a number of potential advantages to the integrated model, their study reached no firm conclusions and this is an area that requires more research.

Case Study Eleven: Oak House, Ipswich, England

Location

Oak House is a new-build extra care scheme that opened in 2004 in a rural part of Suffolk. It is located on the edge of a small village, which has two pubs and a hairdressing salon but no shop. Three miles away is a larger village which has more amenities, including a post office. The nearest city is Ipswich, about six miles (9.6 kilometres) away.

About the scheme

Oak House has 38 flats, eight with two bedrooms and the remainder with one. A specialist dementia care unit sits within the scheme, separated by an additional set of key-fob-controlled security doors. The scheme comprises a single building mainly of wood, brick and glass, with lots of space and natural light. As well as a central residents' lounge there are also several smaller 'pod' lounges near to tenants' flats. The garden is well planted, has ample seating and includes a paved circular walk. Oak House was built to replace a nearby residential care home as part of Suffolk County Council's strategy for older people.

Activities and facilities

The scheme has a wide range of services and facilities, including a restaurant, a hairdressing salon, a laundry, a guest room and assisted bathrooms. A large room is used for day services three days a week, one of these days for people with specific dementia and mental health needs. An activities coordinator is funded half time through Supporting People. Activities include music nights, games and entertainment by local schools.

Staffing and care

The scheme manager is employed by Housing 21, but her post is half funded by social services. An administrative assistant post is part funded by social services and care staff are seconded from social services. Staff operate a system whereby each support worker 'key-works' several tenants and each senior support worker supervises several support workers. District nurses visit once or twice a day, a local GP visits weekly as well as being on call and a local chiropodist makes regular visits. The scheme also has access to a psychogeriatrician. A number of tenants come under a community psychiatric nurse who is also on the allocations panel.

Accessible design is also important in terms of encouraging residents to get physical exercise, which has been shown to have specific benefits for those who are physically frail (Judge et al, 1994), and may increase their ability to perform and maintain activities of daily living. Reduced performance of everyday tasks has in turn been associated with worsening life satisfaction, particularly among those aged 85 and over (Bowling, 1997). In a review of over 90 studies, Gauvin and Spence (1996) found a consistent association between physical activity and psychological wellbeing. This is particularly important in the light of the fact that older people are a high-risk group for depressive symptoms, and depression is recognised as one of the most frequent mental health problems among older people (Blazer, 2003). It can be seen, therefore, that accessible design is important to the overall wellbeing of residents in housing with care schemes as well as their levels of social interaction. This is particularly relevant because of recent evidence of deteriorating wellbeing and worsening mental health for older people in general (Allen, 2008).

'Design principles for extra care housing' (Nicholson, 2008), published by the Housing LIN, provides a comprehensive guide to creating an enabling environment for older people. This highlights the crucial role of design in terms of a range of key aims of housing with care, including allowing individuals to find privacy, comfort, support and companionship and creating a resource for the local community.

6.7 Outdoor spaces

There is a growing recognition of the role of outdoor spaces in promoting quality of life and wellbeing for older people (Chalfont, 2005; Owen, 2006). A range of benefits of having access to appropriate outdoor spaces have been identified, including opportunities for exercise, provision of a varied social environment, sensory stimulation, access to plants and wildlife and therapeutic gardening. A report by Ward-Thompson and Sugiyama (2006) concluded that supportive outdoor spaces can encourage life satisfaction and health for older people by promoting a more active lifestyle. Similarly, a study carried out in Ireland by Leyden (2003) reported that mixed land use and pedestrian–friendly or 'walkable' neighbourhoods can encourage social interaction and cohesion. In addition, living near the main activity centre and sharing enclosed outdoor spaces can increase the likelihood of unplanned encounters and lead to greater 'place attachment' (Sugihara and Evans, 2000).

The Housing LIN design principles for extra care housing outline some of the ways in which outdoor spaces can enable the extension of living space into the garden by, for example, locating terraces and patios alongside a lounge or conservatory (Nicholson, 2008). A range of features are identified as important to the provision of opportunities to use such spaces for social interaction, such as seating, accessible pathways and the creation of pleasant environments through appropriate planting strategies. Many residents have moved from private houses due to, among other reasons, the difficulty of continuing to maintain their gardens. Many of them welcome the opportunity to continue their gardening interests at some level and find it to be a valuable social activity (Vallelly et al, 2006). Such interests are not always catered for in housing with care settings, despite the existence of appropriate outdoor spaces and landscaped grounds. However, some good examples do exist, including the provision of raised beds, accessible greenhouses and allotments. Even where land is in short supply, imaginative solutions can be found, such as the gardening 'plots' that can be found on the roof of the Monica Wills House extra care housing scheme in Bristol, as shown in Photo 3.

Photo 3: Roof gardening at Monica Wills House in Bristol (Photograph by Tamany Baker)

Evans and Means (2007) concluded that accessible design of open spaces was an important factor in encouraging retirement village residents to move around the complex and take part in social activities. They found that certain aspects of the physical layout, such as exposed open spaces, could deter residents from going out and might therefore limit levels of social interaction. This was particularly true for people with impaired mobility. It has also been suggested that cul-de-sacs, a common feature of retirement villages, can encourage neighbourhood interaction (Festinger, 1954). Another study found that the level of traffic in residential streets was a major factor in the development of social lives (Hart, 2008). As a result, the average resident in a street with heavy traffic had less than one quarter the number of local friends and half the number of local acquaintances than someone living on a street with light traffic. In addition, residents of light traffic streets reported almost three times the number of 'gathering spots' than those living on medium or heavy traffic streets. These findings are particularly interesting, given the importance of the neighbourhood to older people, and they highlight one of the attractions of housing with care settings, which tend to be traffic-free environments with plenty of pedestrian-friendly places for social interaction.

A detailed exploration of the evidence for the impact of the outdoor environment can be found in 'Health, place and nature' (Sustainable Development

Commission, 2006). This report identifies a range of factors that can influence health in direct and indirect ways, including natural spaces, noise, air pollution, accessibility, street design and mixed land use. It concludes that for people to be healthy there must be a health-enhancing environment and that communities must be built to be sustainable.

6.8 Services and facilities

As discussed in Chapters Four and Five, retirement communities and extra care housing usually offer a wide range of facilities for residents. These commonly include shops, a restaurant, a beauty salon, a computer room, a gym and landscaped grounds. The Sustainable Development Commission report (2006) suggests that accessible amenities can help promote a sense of community. Similarly, studies of extra care housing (Evans and Vallelly, 2007) and retirement villages (Bernard et al, 2007; Evans and Means, 2007) have concluded that facilities such as these not only support independence for residents but also provide important venues for social interaction and the promotion of 'collectivity'. This supports evidence that older people in general experience considerably greater problems than other age groups in accessing a range of services, as shown in Table 6.1.

Table 6.1: Percentage of age group reporting problems accessing a range of amenities in England (2004–05)

Age of person	Corner shop	Supermarket	Post office	Doctor	Local hospital
16–44	1	1	1	2	6
45–64	1	2	2	2	7
65–74	3	2	3	3	10
75+	7	8	7	7	17

Source: Survey of English Housing 2004–05 (www.communities.gov.uk/housing/housingresearch/housingsurveys/surveyofenglishhousing)

In housing with care schemes, communal lounges are a focal point for social interaction for many tenants and can serve as a venue for a wide range of activities. Some schemes also have smaller 'pod' lounges around the scheme that can create a sense of local 'neighbourhood' for those who live near them. Evans and Vallelly (2007) identified shops and restaurants as particularly important because of their value as venues for social interaction. They described one extra care housing scheme where the restaurant became unviable economically and had to close down, which resulted in residents having to eat pre-cooked meals in their own apartments. They suggest that commissioners should consider subsidising facilities in these circumstances, or possibly explore innovative solutions such as operating restaurants as social enterprises. In their study of Westbury Fields retirement village, Evans and Means (2007) reported that social interaction among residents was centred largely on shared leisure interests and the use of communal facilities. They concluded that the provision of a range of facilities is crucial to a sense of community, largely due to their role as venues for a range of social interactions. Oldenburg (1999) called these semi-public areas the 'third place' and highlighted their importance to neighbourhood social interaction and the health of communities.

6.9 Social activities

Social activities emerge from the literature as important in long-term care settings, largely because they provide one of the main opportunities for social interaction, particularly for residents in poorer health (Croucher et al, 2006). Vallely et al (2006) found considerable differences between the extra care housing schemes in their study in terms of the number and range of activities provided, partly because of different staffing and funding arrangements. They also described two different models for arranging activities – resident led and staff led – and identified a number of potential advantages for each.

Some specific activities have been shown to have an impact in certain settings. For example, regular reminiscence groups can increase self-esteem in nursing homes, and access to the internet can increase social interaction. It is also important to consider that some residents seek solitude rather than social interaction; the important thing is to have the opportunity and choice of whether to interact or not. The *Health survey for England 2000* (Tait and Fuller, 2002) provided some interesting statistics on the involvement of older people in activities. Women in care homes took part in more activities than men, while those over 80 participated less than those aged between 65 and 79. Women and men in good health had similar levels of social participation but, among those with poor health, women were twice as likely as men to take part in activities. These findings have particular implications for housing with care settings, where men are very much in a minority and can become socially isolated. This raises the challenge of providing social activities that are of particular interest to men. Evans and Vallely (2007) highlight an example of such provision in the form of a men's group operating in an extra care housing scheme in Gateshead. This group was attended by male residents and men from the local community. As well as just sitting and chatting, funds had been raised to purchase a pool table and electronic dartboard, both of which were very popular. Residents who attended the weekly group talked very enthusiastically about it, and it seemed to encourage a strong sense of belonging.

Another UK study of people between the ages of 50 and 74 found that overall activity level was associated positively with wellbeing and life satisfaction (Warr et al, 2004). In particular, activities in the family and social sphere and the church and charity domains were found to be important. In contrast, a study of active older people living in the community in the US found that engaging in more activities does not necessarily enhance wellbeing (Everard, 1999). The type of activity was more important and activities engaged in for social reasons were more closely linked to wellbeing than other activities. As with physical exercise, there is some evidence that the impact of social activities may be greatest for people with physical frailties. An American study found that, for older people with functional limitations, maintaining a stable activity level by increasing participation in activities that remained accessible to them (a process known as consolidation) resulted in higher levels of morale compared with those who did not consolidate (Atchley, 1998).

Several studies have looked at specific types of social activity in terms of their impact on wellbeing. One Scottish study found that older people who took part in community singing experienced physical, emotional, social and cultural benefits as well as increased social wellbeing (Hillman, 2002). What is clear from all of these studies is that the opportunity to take part in social activities is central to the development of friendships within housing with care settings.

6.10 Connecting with the wider community

For many people living in housing with care, social networks in the wider community around the scheme are at least as important as those within the housing scheme, often because their previous housing was in the area. Even for those who have moved from further afield, having the opportunity to access social events and activities in the local area can be an important aspect of feeling a sense of belonging to the community.

In the UK a broad range of government initiatives have focused on promoting a sense of community as a way of revitalising neighbourhoods and increasing social cohesion. These include the Active Communities Development Fund, Community Chests, New Deal for Communities, the Transforming Communities Programme, the Safer Communities Housing Fund, the Neighbourhood Renewal Fund and the Community Empowerment Fund, to name just a few. The implications for this focus on a sense of community were detailed in the National Strategy for Housing in an Ageing Society (DCLG, 2008), particularly in terms of inclusive design and an emphasis on integration with local communities. Similarly, initiatives such as the Lifetime Homes Standard, Lifetime Neighbourhoods and Sustainable Communities all create a vision of enabling environments that will be future proofed to meet the needs of people as they age. To a large extent these priorities reflect the World Health Organization Age-Friendly Cities initiative (WHO, 2006), with its focus on social and environmental factors that promote healthy ageing. Taken together, these initiatives outline a number of key elements of communities that support healthy ageing:

- health and wellbeing
- an enabling environment
- access to services and facilities
- integrating with the local community
- supporting diversity.

Eales et al (2008) describe the resources needed to support healthy ageing across three types of environment: natural, human–built and social. These resources include good housing, accessible services, enabling interior and exterior spaces, appropriate transportation, opportunities to maintain relationships with family and friends and opportunities for civic engagement. This section will now explore the potential of housing with care settings to operate as genuine communities and the extent to which they incorporate features that make them age friendly.

A range of factors come into play in terms of enabling a level of connection with the local area. Evans and Vallelly (2007) emphasised the importance of location in general and the effect of rural settings in particular. Housing with care schemes in rural areas often face additional challenges in terms of enabling residents to access their social networks in the local community. The study especially highlighted the challenges to community participation posed by restricted access to public transport, poorly designed and located street furniture and lack of available support staff to facilitate outings. These factors tend to be less of an issue for extra care housing schemes because they tend to be more embedded in existing neighbourhoods and therefore provide relatively good access to social contacts and a range of facilities. However, as discussed in Chapter Four, limited land availability and planning restrictions mean that many UK retirement villages are in rural locations away from large population centres and are therefore more likely to face challenges in terms of enabling residents to stay connected with the communities from which they have come. One possible compromise is to locate a retirement village close to an existing community, as is the case with many recent UK developments that have been built on the edge of villages. This brings a number of potential advantages, as summarised in Case Study Twelve. Physical proximity alone is not sufficient to achieve these potential advantages. It is also important to foster links with the local community, including the provision of physical access for people with mobility problems. Some ways of achieving this are described in Case Study Twelve.

Case Study Twelve: Painswick retirement village, Gloucestershire, England

Background
This private development, which opened in 2005, is situated on the edge of a village in the heart of the Cotswolds, a rural area of England. It aims to cater for people with a range of care and support needs, including visual impairment, deafness, incontinence and moderate memory problems. Applicants must be 55 or older and undergo health and risk assessments before moving in.

Housing and care
The retirement village provides three types of accommodation: independent-living apartments, assisted-living apartments and a nursing care centre. An onsite 24/7 domiciliary care team provides flexible care packages according to the needs of residents.

Photo 4: Painswick retirement village square

Housing staff are on duty 24 hours a day and meals are available in the village restaurant or can be delivered to residents' homes if preferred. The retirement village has strong links with the local community. Of those in the assisted-living apartments, 80% are from Painswick and the wider local area.

Facilities
The retirement village offers a wide range of facilities, including communal lounge, dining room, restaurant, laundry, guest facilities, garden, conservatory, community centre, hobby room, cafe, shop, hairdressing salon, library with internet access and a wellness suite (gym, swimming pool, treatment room and jacuzzi). There is a comprehensive programme of organised activities, including shopping trips, crossword sessions, bridge and other games, computer lessons, a music club and a range of outings. Many of the village facilities and activities are open to local residents and many of the retirement village residents belong to local clubs and societies.

Learning points
Locating a retirement village within an existing community has many potential benefits for residents of the retirement village and those living locally. These include:
• for the retirement village residents:
  – ease of maintaining existing social networks and opportunities for wider social interaction;

- access to a far greater range of services, facilities and leisure activities than can be provided within the village itself;
- opportunities for intergenerational contact, eg with local schools;
- for the local community:
  - having retirement accommodation nearby provides the opportunity to remain near to family and friends rather than leaving the area;
  - the retirement village provides jobs for the local community;
  - the retirement village residents can make local shops and services financially viable;
  - access to facilities and specialist health services in the retirement village.

Source: This case study was initially commissioned by the Housing Learning and Improvement Network and can be found on their website at http://networks.csip.org. uk/IndependentLivingChoices/Housing/, along with a extensive range of resources in relation to housing with care.

Another factor in facilitating access to the local community is the nature of the site on which a scheme sits. Landscapes that are not level can reduce access to scheme gardens and present problems for tenants who want to access local facilities on foot or by wheelchair. Equally important is the implementation of accessible design in the local neighbourhood in terms of facilitating residents' access to social networks and amenities. This includes a range of elements of street design, such as the siting of pedestrian crossings and the provision of dropped curbs for people using mobility scooters.

Integration with the local community is of course not a one-way process, and encouraging people who live nearby into a scheme can be an important way of increasing interaction. This can often be achieved by opening the onsite facilities to the public. This approach works very successfully in many retirement villages and extra care housing schemes, where shops, restaurants, beauty salons and leisure facilities are available for public use. As well as increasing contact between residents and the local community, this arrangement can also help to make facilities financially viable where they might otherwise struggle if used only by scheme residents. However, such arrangements need to be carefully thought out for two reasons. First, the balance between private and semi-private space has been identified as a key factor in place attachment (Skjaeveland and Garling, 1997). Second, one criticism of providing public access to onsite facilities is that the security of residents could be put at risk, particularly those who are 'vulnerable'. 'Progressive privacy' is one solution that has been implemented with some success by Housing 21 in many of its extra care housing schemes. This arrangement divides a scheme into different levels of access so that the public can use a range of facilities while the accommodation areas are protected via key-fob-operated security doors.

Another consideration is the impact of gated communities on integration with the local community. Blandy (2008) discusses the academic debates that have been provoked by gated communities. These tend to be divided between those who claim that the clear physical boundaries that characterise such developments encourage a greater sense of belonging and responsibility, and others who suggest that gating creates a divide between people living inside and those in the local community who feel excluded. The UK 2007 Sustainable Communities Act, with its emphasis on mixed tenure and diversity, would appear to support the arguments against gated communities. Gated retirement villages are few and far between in the UK, although the location of many such developments in isolated rural areas may in fact make them almost as inaccessible as gating. In their study of a gated retirement village in a residential area of a large city in southwest England, Evans and Means (2007) reported that there was little evidence that people in the nearby housing made much use of the onsite facilities. They also found that many village residents appreciated the security that they felt was provided by gating. This is supported by a UK survey (Blandy, 2008) that found that greater security was the main reason for 72% of those who expressed a desire to live in a gated community.

Extra care housing schemes, although not gated, tend to provide a secure environment in which staff are usually aware of visitors to the site and often require them to sign in. However, opening up facilities to the public as discussed above can go a long way towards reducing any feeling of exclusion among local people and has also been found to make for a more 'vibrant' community (Evans and Vallelly, 2007).

6.11 The importance of the model of care delivery

It would appear from the evidence reviewed so far in this chapter that housing with care settings such as retirement villages and extra care housing incorporate many features that are widely believed to contribute towards a sense of community and belonging. In particular, they commonly include design features and facilities that support organised and casual social encounters, both within and beyond the scheme, although rural locations can make this latter aspect something of a challenge. The evidence reviewed so far has also identified certain people as at particular risk of social isolation within such schemes, particularly those with physical frailties or cognitive impairment and single men. For these groups in particular, the way in which care is delivered can be significant. It is perhaps obvious that the care provided within housing with care schemes is central to the overall quality of life of tenants. However, it is also true that for people who are at risk of social isolation due to limited mobility or cognitive impairment, the model of delivery of care can also affect their opportunities for social interaction and therefore the extent to which they feel part of the community. For these residents, care staff can be a major source of social contact, particularly for those who have little or no regular contact with family and friends. This means that the system of care working in operation can be important. For example, some schemes operate a key-worker system whereby one or two care staff regularly support each tenant, while other schemes have a more generic approach. Evans and Vallelly (2007) suggest that the key-worker system offers more opportunity for social interaction through the development of a stronger relationship between residents and staff. Opportunities for staff to interact with residents in a social way may also be limited by the growing trend among care providers towards task-oriented care and particularly the practice of charging by the minute. This means that, in theory, residents should be charged for time that staff spend sitting and chatting with them. Although in practice a more flexible approach is often taken, this is nevertheless a very worrying trend. It also has implications for the ability of care staff to take the time to support tenants who need help in accessing activities and facilities both within the scheme and beyond it in the local community. For example, Evans and Vallelly (2007) describe the situation of an extra care housing resident who often had to eat lunch in her apartment because no staff were available to take her down to the scheme restaurant in her wheelchair. The impact of such restrictions on social interaction is clear given the widespread view that communal eating is an important social activity (Vallelly et al, 2006; Sweetinburgh and King, 2007).

Nolan et al (2004) recognised that the relationships between residents, staff, family, friends and people in residential care settings are central to the social wellbeing of residents and to the development of a feeling of community belonging. They raised concerns about some long-stay and continuing care environments, where activity tends to be centred on the provision of personal care and the meeting of minimal universal needs. As an alternative approach, they suggested that relationship-centred care offers significant advantages in terms of quality of life for older people and their opportunities to interact. Their 'senses framework' identified six dimensions that should be taken into account in the delivery of care: a sense of security, a sense of continuity, a sense of belonging, a sense of purpose, a sense of fulfilment and a sense of significance. They also suggested that care environments should encourage interaction with even the most dependent of patient populations in order to provide meaningful activities that meet the disparate needs of residents.

It is also important to recognise the role of family carers in supporting social interaction and a sense of connection with the local community in housing with care settings. Evans and Vallelly (2007) suggested a number of ways in which this support can be encouraged, including the provision of appropriate guest facilities and maintaining good communication and information between families and housing schemes. This theme is also taken up by Help the Aged in their *My home life project* (Owen, 2006). A range of practical factors are identified in order to support the role of family carers in care homes, including making sure there is a quiet, private place for residents and relatives to talk, arranging times for relatives and staff to discuss any issues and organising an orientation process that allows families to negotiate their role in caring for their relative.

The attitude of care staff and scheme managers is also crucial in determining the extent to which residents have opportunities for social interaction, particularly those with cognitive impairment. Reporting on a longitudinal study of people with dementia in extra care housing, Evans and Means (2007) suggested that staff often adopt a guarded approach to managing risk, largely as a result of societal and organisational preoccupations with risk reduction, leading to policies that focus on risk elimination. As a result, the autonomy of residents is often curtailed, along with their opportunities to take part in social activities. The authors recommend more specialist training for staff so that they can make realistic, person–centred assessments of risk, based on individual needs, abilities and preferences, thus allowing a better balance between maintaining safety and promoting independence. Assistive technologies have great potential to help achieve this by monitoring risky behaviours and taking appropriate action. For example, automated sensors can be used to prevent baths from overflowing, to turn off cookers and to detect unusual movements. In the UK the Department of Health has made older people the key target of telecare planning and implementation through an investment of £80 million. Studies suggest that a quarter of a million care home residents could be supported to live in mainstream or extra care housing through the use of telecare and other support services (Kinsella, 2006). In the US tele-healthcare is routinely made available but only for 60 days for people aged over 65, and its availability for people with long-term conditions is also limited. It is apparent that assistive technology has great potential to maximising independence for older people and thereby provide opportunities for social interaction and community engagement. Both extra care housing and retirement villages provide ideal environments in which these benefits could be realised, due to the economies of scale and the existence of the necessary infrastructure and support systems.

So far the use of assistive technology in these settings has been mainly restricted to basic devices such as community alarms. There are, of course, exceptions. For example, Fold Housing Association in Northern Ireland has incorporated a range of telecare devices into some of its extra care housing, including bed–occupancy sensors, wandering alerts, epilepsy sensors and medication reminders. However, in general much of the implementation has been as pilot schemes and wider coverage would appear to depend on determining and calculating cost savings.

6.12 Place attachment

Chapter Two included a look at some elements of the environment that are thought to promote place attachment, another important dimension of a sense of community. The work of Livingston et al (2008) found that these included many characteristics that are commonly found in housing with care settings, including a large proportion of older people, strong social networks, low levels of crime and a low turnover of residents. Giuliani and Feldman (1993) discussed territoriality as an extreme form of place attachment through the control of space, manifested in not wanting others to use that space and the regulation of social interaction. Could this be part of the attraction of gated retirement schemes? There is certainly evidence from the study by Evans and Means (2007) that many residents felt protective of the space inside the gates, while a review of the literature by Blandy et al (2003) concluded that the psychology of gated communities was one of segregation and escape from crime. These findings also indicate that place attachment generally increases with age. If, as they suggest, attachment stems from local social relationships and these tend to form more easily between people with common backgrounds, interests and lifestyles, then housing with care settings could provide the perfect ingredients for the development of place attachment.

Another factor that has been associated with strong place attachment is the extent to which an individual feels their place of residence is a matter of choice (Sampson, 1988). For most people who live in retirement villages and extra care housing this would seem to be the case. There are, of course, exceptions. Some people who have purchased apartments in a retirement village may find it difficult to move again if the developers are entitled either to a percentage of the sale price or to all of the increased equity, both of which are fairly common arrangements. Similarly, for many people a move to extra care housing is not planned but takes place as a result of a crisis, and the emphasis on supporting independence can be unwelcome. However, given the fact that they are in considerable demand and tend to have waiting lists, it seems safe to assume that the majority of residents in these two settings are there out of choice.

6.13 Conclusion

The concept of 'community' is a major element in marketing campaigns for retirement villages and extra care housing schemes. Evidence from the limited research carried out so far suggests that it is also important to many of the older people who live in them. Community is a complex and disputed concept, but most theories and much of the research suggests that social interaction is the most important factor in creating place attachment and promoting the development of a sense of community. It also seems that fleeting, informal social encounters are at least as important to a sense of community as more established friendships. This means that bringing together people who already have established social networks to live in housing with care settings need not be a barrier to the development of community. It also means that if such schemes are to operate as communities as intended, it is crucial to design the built environment to promote social interaction among those who live there and with the wider community.

Housing with care schemes provide a very distinctive environment and commonly incorporate a range of features that are thought to contribute towards a sense of community. In this chapter I have explored some of these features, including clear physical boundaries, accessible design of indoor and outdoor spaces, a range of facilities and services, the provision of social activities and opportunities to engage with the wider community. I have also highlighted a number of potential barriers to maximising the development of community in housing with care settings. In particular I have discussed the challenges raised by the physical location of some schemes and the difficulties that residents can experience in accessing amenities in the wider community.

Any examination of the marketing and publicity for housing with care schemes leads to the conclusion that one of the main attractions of such environments is the similarity or 'like-mindedness' of residents. However, much of the recent literature suggests that modern communities are just as much about difference and conflict as they are about sameness. The next chapter explores diversity in retirement housing and how it affects the development of a sense of community.

Notes

[1] www.retirementvillages.co.uk

[2] www.retirementvillages.co.uk

SEVEN

Diversity, community and social interaction

7.1 Introduction

Retirement villages are widely marketed as 'communities' for people from similar backgrounds who aspire to similar lifestyles. For example, Roseland Parc in Cornwall, England, tempts potential buyers with the promise that 'The village community atmosphere will allow you to forge new friendships with like-minded people who share your interests, your joys and your challenges in life'.[1] This emphasis on sameness is even more pronounced in the US, where retirement housing schemes are frequently based around a common interest in golf or other leisure activities. Diversity is seldom trumpeted as a selling point, although extra care housing is often more open about supporting people with a range of care needs, largely due to its roots in social care provision. At the same time there is a recognition that the overall housing sector needs to support an ageing population that is increasingly diverse in terms of age, cognitive functioning, mobility, health status, care needs, lifestyles and aspirations.

This chapter explores the extent to which diversity can be supported in housing with care settings and examines how notions of 'like-mindedness' sit with theories of community and government policies that promote 'mixed communities' (see for example ODPM, 2003b). A number of challenges to supporting diversity are identified, including a lack of clear information about the nature of such settings, tensions between residents from different socio-economic backgrounds and a lack of tolerance of different lifestyles. I also discuss the age-segregated nature of most housing and care environments and the implications of this for social cohesion and the concept of community. A range of other factors are identified as important to promoting diversity, including the siting of community facilities, the availability of inclusive activities and accessible design.

The chapter finishes with an analysis of the extent to which the relatively limited diversity found in housing with care schemes fits in with the claims made for them as communities. It also explores the nature of community in age-segregated settings and considers whether specialist housing of this type is an indication of a failure to integrate older people into society.

7.2 Diversity and community theory

Much of the body of theory on 'community' emphasises sameness rather than difference, focusing as it does on common interests, similar lifestyles, collective goals and shared identities. For example, Campbell (1958) suggested that groups are more cohesive where members pursue a common goal, are interpersonally similar and have shared and stable boundaries. However, more recently some commentators have suggested that diversity and difference are important characteristics of community (see for example Brent, 1997; Hoggett, 1997). Abrams and Bulmer (1986) acknowledged that neighbourhoods are not all about harmony and good relations but also contain an element of conflict due to pressures to conform to social norms. This approach is borne out by the findings of a study on immigration and social cohesion carried out in six UK cities (Hickman et al, 2008). Most people interviewed felt that social cohesion was to do with achieving a balance between difference and unity in local areas, rather than expecting complete consensus on values and priorities. It is also reflected in the policies of New Labour, which aim to reverse the breakdown of community and achieve social cohesion by promoting 'mixed' communities of diverse and advantaged/disadvantaged groups. For example, an Urban Task Force report urged the creation of mixed-tenure neighbourhoods to reduce the physical and social barriers between income groups (Rogers, 1999). These, it suggested, are symbolised by the distinctions between social-rented and owner-occupied housing. Similarly, the Sustainable Communities Plan (ODPM, 2003b) identified a number of key features of sustainable communities, including fairness, tolerance, cohesion, respect and engagement with people from different backgrounds, cultures and beliefs. It also suggests that housing can contribute to this mix by encouraging sustainability and promoting social inclusion. The government's National Strategy for Housing in an Ageing Society (DCLG, 2008) spelt out the role of retirement housing in promoting sustainable communities, including the need to support diversity and social interaction. A further sense of urgency in the government's drive towards diversity is the challenge of integrating increasing numbers of immigrants into existing communities.

As mentioned in the introduction to this chapter, diversity is not seen as a strong selling point for retirement villages. Instead, developers tend to emphasise the fact that potential residents will be sharing their living environment with people from similar backgrounds. For example, Denham Garden village in Buckinghamshire has recently been expanded to provide 326 cottages for people aged 55 or more and is being marketed as a 'community of like-minded people' that offers a 'carefree, active existence in your later years'. However, this can be contrasted with the extent to which developers are keen to highlight the suitability of their schemes for people with a wide range of care needs, presumably because this is likely to maximise their market appeal. The rest of this chapter explores the level of diversity that exists in housing with care settings such as retirement villages and extra care housing schemes.

7.3 Health status

A lack of statistics in relation to retirement villages in the UK makes it difficult to compare the health status of residents. However, much of the provision is based on a continuing care model, whereby residents should not have to move unless they require hospital care. Most developments therefore aim to attract residents with a range of care needs, and villages usually offer accommodation and care packages to cater for three levels of dependency. Terminology varies considerably between developers, but these are sometimes called independent-living, 'hotel-style' apartments and nursing care. These are described in Box 7.1.

Box 7.1: Accommodation options in retirement villages

Independent living:
- apartments with one or two bedrooms and a fully equipped kitchen;
- option to purchase personal assistance or care as required;
- use of bookable guest apartment;
- patio or balcony and parking space or garage;
- payment of service charge covers external building maintenance, landscaped grounds, use of facilities and social activities, and so on.

Hotel style or assisted living or close care:
- apartments with one or two bedrooms and a small 'galley' kitchen for preparing hot drinks and snacks;
- provision of daily meals and catering as required;
- personal care assistance for bathing, dressing, and so on, as required;
- 'hotel' services such as cleaning, linen and personal laundry;
- 24-hour onsite staff for planned care and emergency cover;
- activities and transport for outings and visits.

Nursing care:
- full nursing home service, including physical disability and terminal illness;
- provision often includes respite care, convalescence, short-term arrangements and care on a long-term basis;
- may include specialist provision for people with dementia;
- regulated by the Commission for Social Care Inspection.

A small number of research studies have reported on the health status of retirement village residents. The 200 people living in a variety of accommodation at Westbury Fields retirement village in southwest England were found to have a broad range of health care needs in terms of their levels of sensory impairment, mobility problems, mental health needs and continence (Evans and Means, 2007). This is reflected in the fact that a majority of residents cited their own health or that of a spouse as the main reason for moving in. A similar situation was reported at Berryhill retirement village in Staffordshire (Bernard et al, 2004), where nearly three quarters of residents reported having limiting longstanding illness, compared with a national figure of 38.5% of people aged over 50.

The Westbury Fields study (Evans and Means, 2007) is of particular interest here because one of the central aims of the village was to support a diverse population in terms of socio-economic background and levels of dependency. In order to achieve this the village comprised a mixture of publicly funded extra care housing, privately owned apartments and a nursing care home. The authors reported widespread awareness among residents of different backgrounds. One described the set-up as similar to 'a council estate next to a private estate' and felt that diversity in terms of background was irrelevant to the development of the village as a community. Others felt that the village management was trying too hard to achieve social integration across tenures. However, there was evidence that for some private apartment owners the mix of dependency levels within the village was an issue, as expressed by the following quote:

'I don't like being here, I'll be honest, because I don't like being surrounded by decrepit old people. With the best will in the world, you talk to some of them and they don't answer – I've given up trying to hold a conversation.' (Evans and Means, 2007: 45)

However, many residents welcomed the mix of dependency levels within the village, and the research report includes several examples of both formal and informal support taking place between residents in different tenures.

There is a great deal more information available regarding the health care needs of people in extra care housing. An initial report on the evaluation of extra care schemes that received capital funding from the Department of Health[2] found that 64% of residents had a care need, just under 30% had moderate or more severe levels of dependency and 4% were 'severely mentally impaired'. A very small number of residents had no care needs, while 66% were expected to receive home care and 12% were expected to receive more than 14 hours per week. It is interesting to contrast this with retirement villages, where a considerable proportion of residents receive no care package at all.

In the study of social wellbeing in extra care housing (Evans and Vallelly, 2007), it was found that 62% of residents received at least seven hours of personal care per week. In addition 73% used domestic ('home help') services and nearly all residents had meals provided. A survey of all the tenants of Housing 21's 15,000 sheltered and extra care housing schemes (Housing 21, 2007) provided a range of statistics concerning the care needs of residents, including the following:

• 76% had a social services assessed care service;
• 32% had more than 10 hours of personal care per week;
• 82% had some sort of domestic care provision;

- two thirds used mobility aids at least some of the time;
- 67% had a longstanding illness or health condition that affected their activities of daily living;
- 35% had various mental health conditions;
- visual impairment was reported for 11.4% of residents and 39% stated that they had impaired hearing;
- 27% were diagnosed with or suspected of having dementia.

These figures indicate relatively high levels of frailty among extra care residents. This reflects the fact that extra care housing is largely provided by not-for-profit organisations in collaboration with local authorities and focuses at least as much on care needs as it does on housing provision. The statistics also highlight the fact that an increasing proportion of extra care housing residents have dementia, whether diagnosed or not. Dementia currently affects an estimated 700,000 people in the UK, a figure that is predicted to rise to 1.7 million by 2050. If housing with care settings are to support diversity they need to be able to meet the needs of this group of service users. This has been recognised by the UK government in its National Dementia Strategy (Department of Health, 2009), which promotes an integrated approach across health, housing and social care. In the US, government recognition and support of appropriate housing for people with dementia has been less substantial and varies widely from state to state.

Previous work (Evans et al, 2008) has identified several key challenges to supporting people with dementia in housing with care settings. These include design of the built environment, models of care, staff training, the provision of facilities, social wellbeing, a balanced approach to risk and the appropriate use of assistive technologies. The study concluded that housing with care settings have the potential to support people with mild to moderate dementia, but that there are serious questions about what happens to people when their illness becomes more advanced. This is supported by research findings that worsening dementia was a factor for 41% of extra care housing residents who moved to nursing care settings (Vallelly et al, 2006).

There is an ongoing debate about the best way of supporting people with dementia in housing with care settings, with three models commonly being used:

- *Integrated schemes:* these support people with dementia alongside all other residents. Some residents may develop dementia in situ while other schemes will offer vacancies to people who are known to have dementia.
- *Segregated schemes:* in this model people with dementia live in a dementia 'wing', which usually includes separate care staff and facilities. Residents who do not have dementia live in the main part of the scheme.
- *Specialist dementia schemes:* these accommodate only people with dementia.

Vallelly et al (2006) recognised the potential benefits of specialist units in terms of targeting services but they also identified a range of disadvantages. In particular, they questioned the impact of segregated arrangements on social interaction for residents with dementia and the extent to which they might enjoy a sense of being part of a community. This issue has been identified by extra care providers as one of the top priorities for further research.

Many retirement villages are less welcoming of residents with dementia, although there are some exceptions. Some accept people with short-term memory problems but specifically state that they cannot support so-called 'challenging behaviours' or 'wandering'. Those that include onsite nursing care homes can be more flexible, but even these tend to find alternative placements for residents with more advanced dementia (Croucher et al, 2003). Two notable exceptions are Westbury Fields retirement village in Bristol and Buckshaw retirement village in Lancashire, both of which include specialist dementia care services. This sort of arrangement has been shown to have benefits for the partners of village residents who have dementia by enabling them to take part in the village social life environment while remaining close to their partner in the specialist unit (Evans and Means, 2007). A new care village due to be opened in North Somerset in 2010 by the St Monica Trust will include a single-storey, 71-bed self-contained care home that is being built as five smaller, interconnected 'houses'. This design aims to enhance the quality of life for residents with dementia in particular and is based to a large extent on the 'green house' concept.[3] This model is found in the US and New Zealand and aims to address quality of life issues for people living and working in care settings by providing facilities on a domestic scale. Each 'house' accommodates up to 10 people and aims to optimise the size, design and organisation in order to create a 'warm community' based around relationships. An evaluation of this model found that it led to significant increases in self-reported quality of life for residents (Kane et al, 2007). This mirrors research findings showing that smaller residential facilities promote greater community integration for adults with intellectual disability (Heller et al, 1998).

The provision of activities that are accessible to residents with a range of physical and cognitive abilities has also been shown to be important in terms of supporting diversity in extra care housing (Evans and Vallelly, 2007). However, the same study also found a lack of understanding and tolerance of diversity among residents with the lowest care and support needs.

7.4 Ethnic background

In general, the provision of services does not reflect the diversity of local populations in Britain. For example, minority ethnic groups make up 22% of the population but only 1% of this group use traditional social services (Bartlett and Leadbetter, 2008). A review by Croucher et al (2006) concluded that there was a paucity of detailed research into housing with care for black and minority ethnic (BME) elders (elders is the commonly used terminology). There is, however, a reasonable body of evidence of various types suggesting a lack of provision. For example, Patel (1999) highlights a shortage of residential provision for Chinese elders in London. In terms of older people's housing this disparity may be partly due to differences in age profiles. For example, in 1991 only 3% of people of pensionable age in the UK were from BME groups. A report by Age Concern (Jones, 2006) identified the potential of extra care housing to promote the inclusion of South Asian elders and called on local authorities and providers to target BME groups specifically as residents. However, there are considerable barriers to achieving this, including addressing the stigma attached to all types of supported housing among South Asian leaders and providing appropriate information about the range of housing available. Jones (2006) identified 12 extra care schemes specifically targeted at ethnic groups. This represented 427 units in total nationally, over half of which were located in the West Midlands. He concluded that overall there is relatively little extra care provision targeted at BME elders. He also described a review of housing for BME elders in Bristol that outlined the need for schemes providing 'small, shared cultural and language groupings' as a way of overcoming cultural isolation and social stigma. Several schemes like this have now been developed, including Tia Hua Court in Middlesbrough. This scheme was developed by Middlesbrough Council and Tees Valley Housing Group as part of a plan to develop a 'mini Chinatown', to include a new community centre and commercial units alongside housing for older people. Close collaboration with the local Chinese community took place in order to ensure that cultural needs were incorporated in the design. For example, there is no apartment 4, which is seen as an unlucky number, and all apartments are connected to a Chinese satellite TV channel.[4]

This and other developments demonstrate a successful approach to designing extra care housing that meets the needs of specific BME groups. However, it is difficult to find examples of ethnic diversity within schemes and the proportion of residents from BME backgrounds tends to be non-existent or extremely low. For example, one study of eight extra care schemes reported that of the 446 residents only 13 were non-white (Darton et al, 2008). One attempt to provide ethnically diverse extra care housing is Sonali Gardens in the Tower Hamlets area of London. This scheme was primarily developed to meet the needs of Bangladeshi and Asian elders, who make up half the population of the local ward, but was also intended as 'a mixed community' for anyone who could benefit from its particular kind of environment and needed at least 12 hours of care a week (Brenton, 2005). The scheme initially suffered somewhat from being misrepresented in the local press as an 'Asians-only estate'. Another example comes from Colliers Court, an extra care scheme in Bristol, where it was originally intended that 10 of the 50 flats would be allocated to Chinese elders. This proved difficult due to the eligibility criteria for extra care, so eventually the 10 flats were rented to Chinese elders as 'standard' sheltered housing. These examples serve to illustrate some of the challenges of providing diversity in extra care housing and the need for commissioners to carry out comprehensive consultation with the wider community.

7.5 Socio-economic background

Another aspect of diversity in retirement housing, and one that has been the subject of considerable debate, is socio-economic background. Many of the criticisms of housing with care in general and retirement villages in particular have focused on equity and choice. For example, Phillipson (2007: 330) suggested that there were 'significant inequalities between those older people who are able to make decisions about where and with whom to live, and those who feel marginalised and alienated by changes in the communities in which they had aged in place'. Retirement village residents would for the most part seem to fall firmly into the category of those older people who are able to make choices about where they live.

Chapter Two highlighted the UK government's aspiration to embrace 'sustainable' communities that promote social and economic diversity and avoid the perceived negative effects of concentrations of wealth and deprivation. The National Strategy for Housing in an Ageing Society (DCLG, 2008) makes it clear that for retirement housing this means providing mixed tenure in specialist developments. This approach appears to be based largely on the assumption that social mixing through residence in the same place can help to achieve social cohesion while also reducing anti-social behaviour. This is a far from new idea. One of the first planned mixed communities was Bournville estate, established by George Cadbury in 1879, with a mix of owner-occupiers, renters and employees of different statuses. In the late 19th century this new approach to urban planning based on the ideal of self-contained 'balanced' communities, often described as 'garden cities', became popular in several countries.

Mixed tenure commonly provides three options: outright ownership, shared ownership and rental. However, the evidence base for the impact of mixed tenure on the development of a sense of community is varied. A review of the literature from several countries (Sarkissian et al, 1990) concluded that, while the concept of socially mixed communities is very resilient, the balance of evidence suggests that it is unworkable in practice and can actually discourage meaningful interaction. One study of general housing estates found that, while social contact between residents gradually increased over time, most estates were not characterised by inclusive social networks. It also concluded that the formation of mixed communities was constrained by the physical separation of tenures (Kearns and Mason, 2007). This was largely because most residents only got to know their close neighbours. A review of the literature from Britain and Holland found little evidence of social interaction between residents from different tenures, largely because lifestyle factors were more important to residents than whether they owned or rented (Kleinhans, 2004). Similarly, a review of the literature by Kleinhans (2004) found little evidence of social interaction across tenures.

In contrast, a review of seven UK research studies (Holmes, 2006) concluded that mixed-income communities can be successful in terms of promoting relations between people from different backgrounds and tenure, as well as improving enhanced neighbourhood satisfaction and quality of life. A study of housing estates in the Notting Hill area of London supported mixed tenure as a way of promoting social mixing (Page and Boughton, 1997). An interesting exploration of place attachment in Guildford, southern England (Uzzell et al, 2002) suggested that social mix does influence social cohesion but that mixed tenure may only support place attachment in neighbourhoods where home ownership is dominant but not overwhelming. A figure of about 60% home ownership was thought to be optimal.

Most of the early extra care housing in the UK was developed by housing associations and was therefore for rental only. In comparison, almost half of the extra care schemes approved by the Department of Health in recent years have been mixed tenure, although there still tends to be a far greater proportion of rental properties in extra care housing. This trend is also reflected in the retirement village sector. Although one of the first UK retirement villages, Hartrigg Oaks, was a mixed-tenure model, most early schemes were private developments and tended towards owner-occupier models. There are many reasons for this move towards mixed tenure. One major driver, as already discussed, is the fact that the government sees mixed communities as a force for social cohesion and is therefore encouraging such arrangements through funding criteria and planning permissions. This trend also reflects a desire to meet demand for older people's housing at a time when the number of owner-occupiers is increasing and the amount of social-rented housing is decreasing. Mixed tenure also offers developers a number of financial advantages, be they private or registered social landlords. For example, the money generated by sales can immediately be used by private developers to reduce borrowing or, in the case of social housing, to subsidise the costs of the rental units. Another recent development is the inclusion of shared ownership in retirement housing schemes through schemes such as HomeBuy.[5]

King and Mills (2005) suggested that mixed tenure raises a set of new and complex issues for developers and managers. This is partly because housing associations acting as developers often have little or no experience of retirement housing for sale, while private developers frequently lack experience of dealing with older people who are eligible for income support or housing benefits. In addition, there is the added complication of the provision of care, often by an organisation other than the landlord. Several not-for-profit organisations have now moved into the retirement village sector and are starting to offer a range of tenures. However, much of the research carried out so far has focused on single-tenure schemes and there has been very little research into mixed tenure in housing with care settings in the UK.

One exception is Evans and Means' (2007) study of a retirement village in southwest England. This development aimed to attract a diverse population from different socio-economic backgrounds by offering three different housing tenures: privately owned retirement apartments, a nursing care home and an extra care housing facility. Crucially, the village adopted a segregated tenure arrangement, with owner-occupied apartments situated in small clusters around the village, the extra care housing located in a large building in one corner of the site and the nursing care home in another corner. There was evidence of limited cross-tenure interaction of a casual, everyday nature, while much of the social interaction within tenures was based around organised activities, such as the croquet club. There were contrasting views among residents as to whether the village functioned as a community. For example, one care home resident described it as 'a real community of very diverse people to mix with' (p 42), while a tenant of the extra care housing commented: 'I don't really regard myself as being part of a community, simply because I don't know any of the other people here'. (p 42)

The interesting point in terms of mixed tenure was that residents tended to identify with the area of the village in which they lived rather than with the village as a whole. For example, one extra care tenant commented: 'I think this, the sheltered housing [extra care] side, has got quite a community spirit going, yes, but I don't think we have a real community spirit with the two sides (p 42)'. There was also a recognition that perceived differences in socio-economic background, as manifested in tenure, were the main factor in patterns of social interaction.

It is important to acknowledge that the village was at an early stage, having been fully open for about 18 months. This raises questions about how long it takes for a sense of community to develop and should be seen in the light of a suggestion by Campbell (1958) that members of newly created neighbourhoods tend to focus much more on establishing similarities than on exploring differences. The view of different areas of the village as distinct and separate was widely reflected in the respondents' expressions. For example, several used the term 'the village' to describe the areas containing the owner-occupied apartments rather than the village as a whole. One resident described those living in owner-occupied apartments as 'that lot up there' and extra care residents as 'us down here' (Evans and Means, 2007 p 42).

In common with other studies (see for example Evans and Vallelly, 2007), communal facilities and spaces were found to be important venues for social interaction. Several village facilities and activities were based in the extra care housing, partly as a way of encouraging cross-tenure interaction. However, this had achieved limited success and had exacerbated feelings of resentment among people living in the owner-occupied retirement apartments, who felt excluded from some of the facilities. This situation was compounded by perceived differences in the financial contribution made by residents of the retirement apartments and those living in extra care housing. The study concluded that achieving the laudable aim of creating a 'mixed' retirement village was hampered by the clustering of tenures, which appeared to discourage social interaction between residents from different areas. This was aggravated by the layout of the site, including the positioning of a cricket pitch at the centre of the village, which created a barrier between tenures. This was particularly true for those with impaired mobility, many of whom felt that it restricted their opportunities to access facilities and take a full part in some aspects of village life. In the context of current theoretical debates of community (see for example Gilleard and Higgs, 2000; Forrest and Kearns, 2001), the fact that tenures occupied separate physical areas of the village exacerbated the differences in social backgrounds and interests.

These messages have been taken on board in the subsequent scheme by the same developer, a mixed-tenure extra care housing scheme that adopts a 'pepperpotting' approach. Under this arrangement, owner-occupier and rental flats are integrated throughout the scheme rather than being clustered together. Although some developers have been concerned that this layout can affect the value of schemes and deter private owners from buying, the evidence suggests that this can work well, particularly if a 'tenure-blind' approach is adopted. This involves using the same design for both owned and rented flats so that they are indistinguishable (Rowlands et al, 2006).

7.6 Gender and sexuality

The gender profile of housing with care residents tends to mirror that of the population in general and reflects the differences between men and women in life expectancy. For example, one study of a UK retirement village reported that 69% of residents were women (Bernard et al, 2004), while in another the figure was 61% (Evans and Means, 2007). The resident profile is similar in extra care housing, with one provider reporting that 69% of their residents are female (Housing 21, 2007). Housing 21 also found that increasing numbers of men are moving into extra care housing. Our study of social wellbeing (Evans and Vallelly, 2007) highlighted the reluctance of men to take part in social activities and identified some examples of good practice in terms of providing for their interests.

Sexual orientation is one area in which there are few if any figures for the residents of housing with care. Chapter Five included an exploration of the increasing interest in gay and lesbian retirement villages in the US. This reflects figures indicating that there are 3 million gay and lesbian seniors currently living in the US, a number that is expected to more than double over the next 25 years. It also suggests that many gay seniors find traditional retirement communities unprepared or unwilling to meet their needs. The research evidence into the experiences and aspirations of GLBT groups is limited but some studies have been carried out in the US. Cahill and South (2002) reported a survey carried out in New York State that found that openly gay and lesbian older people were not welcome in state-funded senior centres. They concluded that current policies and practices in all sectors, including housing with care, compromise the quality of life for GLBT elders in their retirement years. Amendments to the US 1968 Fair Housing Act banned anti-GLBT discrimination in retirement housing. A survey of older gays and lesbians in the US found that a large majority were interested in planned retirement housing specifically sensitive to their needs and many expressed a willingness to relocate significant distances in order to live in such schemes (Lucco, 1987). Interestingly, the respondents were more likely to live alone, to be still working and to have a higher socio-economic status than the general older population. Another US study (Johnson et al, 2005) reported that GLBT adults indicated a strong desire for the development of exclusive GLBT, or GLBT-friendly, retirement care facilities. This was largely due to perceptions of retirement care facilities as potential sources of discrimination on the part of the administration, care staff and residents.

There is much anecdotal evidence for practices that discriminate against gay and lesbian groups. Cahill and South (2002) quote the following shocking example: a nursing assistant enters a room without knocking and sees two older male residents engaging in oral sex. The assistant notifies her supervisor and the two are separated immediately. Within a day, one man is transferred to a psychiatric ward and placed in restraints. A community health board holds that the transfer was a warranted response to 'deviant behaviour'. A series of articles in an American magazine describes some of the discrimination and social isolation experienced by gay people in retirement housing and care environments (Ochalla, 2007).

The first US gay retirement village opened in the 1990s. An article (Shankle et al, 2003) described five such developments in 2003 and several have been opened or planned since then. However, as Cahill and South (2002) point out, most of these are only an option for people with a high income level. There are recent reports that some GLBT retirement schemes are experiencing difficulties attracting sufficient residents and have rebranded themselves as 'gay-friendly' in an attempt to broaden their appeal. This has led to some concerns among gay and lesbian residents (Colker, 2007), who now worry that they might be outnumbered by heterosexual residents. The picture is further complicated because some states bar housing discrimination based on sexual orientation.

Some gay-friendly schemes are starting to emerge in other countries. For example, a British newspaper (Smee, 2008) reported on an old people's home in Berlin that caters exclusively for gays and lesbians, reflecting the fact that 'most gay and lesbian residents keep themselves hidden'. The first Australian retirement village of this type received planning permission in 2008. Given the relatively small number of retirement villages in the UK, it is perhaps not surprising to find that this market has not yet been catered for. Research commissioned by the DCLG (Croucher, 2008) did mention future care and housing as an issue for older lesbians and gay men, partly due to concerns about possible homophobic attitudes among staff and residents of specialist housing. However, the report concludes that very little research has explored the needs and aspirations of older people from the GLBT community in England. This is an area that deserves a great deal more research interest in the future. Meanwhile, it is logical to conclude that the residents of housing with care settings reflect the general population of older people in terms of sexual orientation, although there is no attempt so far to meet their specific needs.

7.7 Age segregation and diversity

Perhaps the most obvious criticism that can be aimed at retirement housing in terms of diversity is its age profile. The fact is that most if not all retirement villages and extra care housing schemes have a lower age limit of around 55, although in some cases it is slightly lower for people who are disabled. In many schemes the leasehold and tenancy agreements are strict about this, with some even specifying a maximum numbers of days a year for which younger people can stay as guests. There are several reasons for such age restrictions in retirement housing. The first of these applies mainly to the US, where the age discrimination law makes an exception for housing that is classified as being exclusively for seniors. In some states such developments are also exempt from planning restrictions and local taxes, such as contributing funds to local schools. For extra care housing the age limit has come about partly as a result of funding arrangements, whereby schemes are developed in collaboration with local authorities and are tied in with older people's strategies and housing-related support budgets. However, one of the main justifications for age-segregated retirement housing is often the perception that it is what older people want. The evidence for this assertion is mixed. An analysis of national data from the US showed that all age groups expressed a preference for social interaction with other age groups (Daum, 1982).

A body of evidence for the impact of age segregation is being developed. One UK study found that whether the effect of age segregation in sheltered housing was positive or negative depended on how it affected residents' self-esteem (Percival, 2001). However, a US study comparing age-segregated and age-integrated housing found that there were differences in contact patterns (Sherman, 1975). In particular, age-segregated residents had less interaction with their children, grandchildren and other relatives, while fewer had friends younger than 40. They also visited neighbours and same-age friends more often. Certainly, the potential benefits of intergenerational contact within society are evident. For example, grandparents are by far the largest source of childcare, accounting for 26% of the total, compared with 10% by family and friends and 17% as formal day care (Prime Minister's Strategy Unit (PMSU), 2008). The economic benefits of this are enormous, but so too are the positive effects on older people in terms of a sense of purpose (Lee, 2006). A study of intergenerational programmes in a range of settings across Spain identified personal and social benefits for both young and old, as well as for the community and society in general (Sanchez, 2008).

A study of housing decisions in later life reported mixed views concerning the advantages and disadvantages of living alongside other older people (Clough et al, 2004). While there was a widespread desire for some of the features of age-segregated settings, such as feelings of safety and less daily worries, some older people wanted to enjoy these features in an intergenerational setting. For others, not wanting to be a burden to their children was a factor in choosing an age-segregated environment. Evans and Means' (2007) study of a UK retirement village found that some residents felt that the lack of younger people prevented the village from being a community. One resident commented, 'It still doesn't feel like a community. It can't, can it, when it's all one age?' (p 46). Another described how, when her grandchildren visited her and played outside, other residents had complained about the noise. However, some saw the age restrictions as a positive feature of the village, including one who said:

> 'If you're not 100%, you know that the other person isn't 100%, so you can talk about it and tell one another and we don't want to be interspersed with lots of young people who wouldn't understand.'
> (Evans and Means, 2007: 46)

Fear of crime is frequently mentioned as a reason for the popularity of retirement villages and this was also one of the factors mentioned by residents of this village. This perception is not supported by the facts, which record that statistically young people suffer more crime by adults than the other way round (Brown, 1995). It may be, however, that such perceptions are fuelled by media portrayals of young people – often described as 'hoodies' – as perpetrators of crime and therefore responsible for the disintegration of community values. One thing that is clear is the need for more research in this area. A range of projects have aimed to increase intergenerational contact in housing settings. For example, the Thinking Village project used the community philosophy approach in order to encourage conversations between young and old people in a neighbourhood of York. Porter and Seeley (2008) commented on the potential benefits of this approach, including increased understanding and tolerance. However, they also concluded that considerable resources are required in order for these benefits to be reflected in everyday life.

7.8 Conclusion

The picture is mixed in terms of the ability of housing with care settings to support diversity. Most retirement villages and extra care housing are based on a continuing care model whereby residents have a 'home for life' and only have to move if they require hospital care. The limited amount of evidence available suggests that most retirement villages do support a range of levels of care needs across a range of accommodation. One exception to this is people with more advanced dementia, who are seldom well supported in such settings and frequently move to nursing care. This situation is slowly changing with the growing interest in new innovations in dementia care, particularly the 'green house' model. Extra care housing tends to target older people with higher levels of care needs, largely because it is often developed in collaboration with local authorities which have social care responsibilities. Most schemes therefore include a minimum number of care hours in their entry criteria. This means that the overall dependency level is higher in extra care housing schemes than in retirement villages, which are almost exclusively private developments and where a significant proportion of residents have no care needs when they move in. This is increasingly the case because of a trend towards people moving into retirement villages at a younger age, particularly in the US, where many schemes are based around leisure interests such as golf.

The limited statistics available suggest that housing with care settings are less successful in supporting diversity in terms of ethnic background. Even after taking into account the different age profiles of BME groups, there appears to be a lack of provision. As already discussed, some recent attempts to target these groups have raised a number of challenges, including the stigma attached to non-family forms of caring. Another increasingly important diversity issue is meeting the needs of older people from GLBT groups. Although there are indications of considerable demand for housing with care settings that are gay and lesbian friendly, this is a relatively new niche market for retirement villages in the US. Provision remains low there and virtually non-existent elsewhere, but this is an aspect of diversity that is likely to see increased attention.

There has been a major drive in recent years to promote neighbourhoods that are mixed in terms of the socio-economic backgrounds of residents, largely as a way to increase social cohesion and reduce anti-social behaviour. This strategy has been reflected in housing with care settings by a shift towards developing schemes that incorporate a mix of tenures, including rental, owner-occupying and shared ownership. This approach has some financial advantages for developers but it also brings new challenges in terms of scheme management. However, the evidence base for promoting mixed communities is weak and there is a particular dearth of evidence in relation to housing with care settings. The little research that has been carried out suggests that the design of the built environment is a key element in promoting cross-tenure social interaction, particularly for residents with poor health or restricted mobility.

The aspect of diversity in housing with care settings that has attracted most criticism is its age-segregated nature, including the now infamous labelling of retirement villages as 'glorified playpens for older people' (Kuhn, 1977). Not surprisingly, the evidence suggests that age segregation leads to less interaction on the part of residents with children, but more interestingly this also extends to other relatives. There is evidence from studies of both extra care housing and retirement villages to suggest that diversity is not welcomed by all residents, while others see it as crucial to being a 'real' community. The data I have presented in this chapter lead to the conclusion that there is less diversity in housing with care settings than in the population in general and therefore, by implication, less than for older people living in the wider community.

The crucial question for this book, then, is how does this affect the potential for such settings to function as communities? Low and Altman (1992) argue that attachment to place is central to social cohesion because it provides a sense of security, helps maintain individual and group identity and fosters self-esteem. The relative homogeneity of housing with care settings does tend to lead to common interests and goals among residents, both factors that are suggested by the research literature as contributing towards cohesive groups. Similarly, many of the factors that promote place attachment, which is also often mentioned as a key factor in promoting a sense of community belonging, can be found in retirement villages and extra care housing. These include opportunities for social interaction, well-defined physical boundaries, good-quality housing and a stable population of older people. A study carried out in England concluded that people factors were more important than place factors in explaining an overall sense of attachment (Gosschalk and Hatter, 1996). The obvious question is whether any age-limited community can be truly diverse. Several writers have argued that age segregation is closely connected to ageism, both as cause and effect.

If we adopt a perspective that views broad diversity, including ethnic and intergenerational mix, as important to a sense of community, then housing with care settings struggle to qualify. However, it is much easier to argue that they are successful as neighbourhoods where social cohesion is based on perceived similarities rather than difference. This argument makes sense in the context of evidence for the increasing importance of neighbourhood attachment as people grow older. It also complements the conclusions of two recent studies of retirement villages: first, that attempts to place people from different backgrounds together and expect them to interact socially could be seen as misguided (Evans and Means, 2007); and second, that equating the success of retirement villages with achieving a balance between fit and frail residents is simplistic and erroneous (Bernard et al, 2007). Finally, it supports suggestions from the literature that the interest in achieving social mix within neighbourhoods stems from nostalgia, utopian ideals and a belief in diversity for diversity's sake.

If we accept that housing with care schemes are best conceived as neighbourhoods, the key question then becomes, how do housing with care schemes as neighbourhoods relate to the wider communities in which they exist? This issue is explored in the concluding chapter of the book.

Notes

[1] www.retirementvillages.co.uk/our-villages/current-villages/Roseland-Parc/Living-Here.aspx

[2] www.pssru.ac.uk/projects/echi.htm

[3] More information on this model can be found at www.ncbcapitalimpact.org/default.aspx?id=148

[4] Further details can be found in a Housing LIN case study at http://networks.csip.org.uk/IndependentLivingChoices/Housing/Topics/browse/HousingOlderPeople/BMEGroups/

[5] Information about the HomeBuy scheme is at www.communities.gov.uk/housing/buyingselling/ownershipschemes/homebuy/

EIGHT

Changing communities and older people

8.1 Introduction

The social and economic structure of local communities in Britain has changed considerably in recent decades, particularly in terms of the closure of services and facilities that have traditionally been at their centre, such as post offices, banks and local shops. These changes affect us all, but they are particularly significant for older people, many of whom spend more time in their neighbourhoods as they grow older and often find themselves facing reduced mobility, poorer health, decreasing incomes and limited opportunities for social interaction. This chapter considers how communities have changed for older people and how they might continue to do so during the coming decades. This includes a look at a range of factors that affect community engagement, including demographic changes, the delivery of low-level services, increasing use of technology and telecare, transport infrastructure, the supply and design of housing, and older people's needs and aspirations. Finally, the future of housing with care settings as communities is explored.

8.2 Older people, social changes and community engagement

While it is important not to treat older people as a homogeneous group, there is a widespread feeling that the so-called baby boomers are different from previous generations. In particular, they are seen as more comfortable with asserting their rights and also have more spending power. The perception of older people as consumers with, on average, greater than ever amounts of money to spend has been well documented (Gilleard and Higgs, 2000). However, it is important to bear in mind that many pensioners are in poverty and, despite ever-increasing consumer choices, the best prices are often only available via the internet or in out-of-town malls. In either case, many older people lack the necessary transport or internet facilities to access them.

There is considerable evidence, much of it reviewed in Chapter Six of this book, to suggest that a sense of community and independence both factor strongly in decisions about where to live in retirement. I have also suggested that the local area in which older people live is of particular importance. As a result, changes in local communities and neighbourhoods often have more impact on older people than they do on many other residents. The next part of this chapter considers some of the social and economic changes that have taken place in recent years and the implications of these changes for older people, particularly in terms of the extent to which they have opportunities to engage with their local community.

The way in which services are delivered has changed greatly in recent years, with a strong trend towards the closure of local outlets. For example, in the UK over 4,000 bank branches closed between 1995 and 2003, 2,500 post offices closed during 2007 and 2008, and 1,409 pubs closed during 2007. A range of other services are under threat, including local shops, garages, police stations, schools, job centres, hospitals, general practices and churches. These closures reduce opportunities for social interaction and can have a major impact on the existence of a sense of community. The effect is particularly strong in rural areas where social life is often focused around local services, which have been hit especially hard. Research carried out by a national newspaper demonstrates that the effect of such changes is particularly evident in rural areas. For example, one area of Yorkshire in northern England has lost 77 services since 2000, including six primary schools, 28 post offices and 25 banks and building societies (Hill, 2008). Similarly, 79 primary and 11 secondary schools have closed in rural England since 2000.

At the same time, there is increasing interest in rural living, with over 800,000 Britons a year moving from city to countryside. This trend is driven by a range of factors, including increased opportunities to work from home, improved broadband internet access and fears of urban crime. Ironically there is a danger that this exodus is threatening the very lifestyle that these migrants are seeking, with rising house prices forcing out local families who have traditionally supported local shops, pubs and schools. According to this argument, these villages are rapidly becoming ghettoes for older people and the rich. A counter-argument suggests that those who hold such sentiments are clinging to an outdated and idyllic notion of village life and that these trends are merely a reflection of wider social changes. Certainly, some villages are rising to the challenge through innovative ideas such as raising funds to build communal facilities, building affordable housing and forming associations with nearby villages in order to share amenities.

There is strong evidence that access to a range of services is a major barrier for older people in particular, as Table 6.1 (on page 81) demonstrates. The recent decision by the UK government to provide free bus transport for older people and with the development of accessible transport strategies are both very welcome developments. However, the limited amount of public transport in rural areas and financial threats to community transport schemes continue to present a major challenge for older people in rural areas.

Similarly, cuts in the provision of adult education seem to have hit older people particularly hard. Research by the National Institute of Adult Continuing Education (Aldridge and Tuckett, 2007) shows that just 9% of over-65s and 7% of over-75s are active learners compared with an average of 20% across the population. At the same time participation in further education funded by the learning and skills councils between 2004 and 2005 fell by almost 25% among the over-60s.

A report by Help the Aged (2008b) highlighted a range of ongoing social and economic changes that are likely to affect older people in a number of ways. For example, increased flooding as a result of climate change is likely to have a disproportionately negative impact on older people who live in high flood-risk areas because of their dependence on their local neighbourhood and the fact that they tend to be particularly sensitive to the disruption of moving. On the other hand, the drive towards more efficient energy use could benefit older people by reducing their heating bills, and better investment in public transport in order to reduce car-produced greenhouse gases could help older people in particular. Similarly, the report speculates that older people might be able to sell their carbon allowances to improve their financial situation. Such scenarios also raise the interesting possibility that some of the local services that have been subject to closure could be reintroduced in order to reduce transport-related pollution, which would benefit older people especially.

The UK government's aim to make housing more ecologically friendly, including the building of 'eco-towns', may offer some advantages to older people due to the fact that many of the features that make places more ecologically sustainable, such as good public transport and well-insulated homes, can also make them more accessible to older people. However, achieving these advantages is dependent on making such places 'age-friendly' environments that can enable and empower older people rather than exclude them. In this context a range of environmental factors such as levels of traffic and pollution are likely to become more important factors in decisions that older people make about where to live. For example, the amount of traffic on the streets has been shown to have a major impact on the social lives of residents (Hart, 2008). This is particularly important since the number of cars on British roads is predicted to increase by 21% to 5.7 million cars by 2031 (Department for Transport, 2005).

Broader economic changes are also having an impact on the lives of older people. For example as people in many Western societies are becoming wealthier on average, it is increasingly difficult to recruit people to caring jobs. At the same time, informal care patterns are changing as more young people move away from the areas in which they grew up because of housing prices and increased social mobility. Such changes can threaten older people's independence and their ability to enjoy opportunities for community engagement.

Many of the changes in methods of access to services and amenities are in direct contrast to recent government policies and strategies, which seek to support independence for older people in the community. For example, in the UK the government's National Strategy for Housing in an Ageing Society (DCLG, 2008) recognises the importance of neighbourhood design for older people in promoting independence and providing opportunities for involvement in the local community. An important aspect of the sustainable communities agenda is the emphasis on the role of neighbourhoods in meeting the needs of existing and future residents, including the provision of facilities and services. If local services and facilities continue to close at the current rate this sustainability will be increasingly difficult to achieve. Similarly, the World Health Organization's Global Age Friendly Cities initiative (WHO, 2006) stresses the importance of social and environmental factors in promoting healthy ageing and enabling access to services and facilities.

Both of these initiatives, which were explored in Chapter Six of this book, contain excellent examples of how neighbourhoods can be age proofed to prevent older people from becoming isolated. In terms of everyday living, characteristics of the built environment such as the quality of pavements, the availability of public toilets and the provision of seating are all of great importance to older people. For example, the incidence of incontinence increases with age and is experienced by up to 6 million people in the UK. The provision of adequate toilets is therefore a major factor in the confidence of many older people to leave their homes and venture out into the local community. However, progress in implementing many of the ideas promoted in these initiatives seems to be slow and the provision of seating and toilets remains far from adequate in some towns. Indeed, there are many examples of such facilities actually being removed, often as a result of vandalism and perceived misuse. This situation requires creative solutions to such problems rather than ill-thought-out actions that disadvantage older people, who have a right to enjoy communal spaces and who should be supported as vital customers for local businesses. Equally, many older people are unable to make full use of their free bus passes because of physical disabilities that prevent them from getting to the bus stop or from getting on and off the bus.

Recent legislation does suggest that the UK government is keen to give citizens more say about what goes on in their local area. For example, both the 2007 Local Government and Public Involvement in Health Act and the establishment of local area agreements devolve more decision making to local areas. In addition, the 2007 Sustainable Communities Act gives greater powers to local citizens to play a role in improving their communities and to challenge decisions that affect them. Older people have a history of high levels of involvement in local governance and it is to be hoped that these initiatives will help them to improve their local environments in ways that support community engagement. *Towards common ground*, the Help the Aged manifesto for lifetime neighbourhoods (Help the Aged, 2008c), suggests 10 key factors that should be taken in to account in order to achieve this, as summarised in Box 8.1.

8.3 Technology and older people

Some of the greatest social changes in recent years have come in the area of technology. For example, the way that information is distributed and services are delivered has radically altered, and access to the most comprehensive information and advice is now via the internet, on both government and private websites. Similarly, many of the best consumer bargains can only be accessed via internet shopping, while digital television – which is being rolled out across the UK – has the potential to provide a range of services, such as making GP appointments and arranging repeat prescriptions. In addition, a broad range of devices, widely

Box 8.1: Help the Aged's manifesto for lifetime neighbourhoods

Lifetime standards
All new homes should be built to meet the Lifetime Homes Standard in order to make it easy for older people to get their homes adapted to meet their changing health needs.

Transport
There should be an alternative to the bus pass so that older people with mobility difficulties can maintain their independence.

Pavements
All pavements should be smooth, non-slip and in good repair so that older people have less fear of falling.

Public toilets
Good public toilets should be available in all neighbourhoods to help reduce the risk of people with incontinence becoming housebound.

Seating
The provision of public seating is essential in supporting older people to use their neighbourhood.

Age-friendly streets
Streets that are safe, clean and well kept are particularly important to older people, who are more likely to fear crime.

Local facilities
Everyone should have access to money, health care and basic food shops within a reasonable distance of their home.

Public spaces
Spaces are vital as venues for people to meet and take part in activities, for example public park, community centre, library.

Information and advice
Information and advice are crucial to older people so that they can access a range of local services, facilities, opportunities and support.

Involvement
Older people's voices need to be heard so that they can take part in local decision making.

known as 'assistive technology', have become available in recent years, with the overall aim of maximising independence for older people. A research briefing issued by the Social Care Institute for Excellence (Beech and Roberts, 2008) provides a useful way of categorising these according their intended function as outlined in Box 8.2 below.

Box 8.2: Categories of assistive technology, according to function

1. supportive technologies for helping individuals perform tasks that they may find difficult (for example, video entry systems, and medication reminder units);
2. detection and reaction (responsive) technologies to help individuals manage risks and raise alarms (for example, unburned gas detectors and panic buttons/pendants);
3. prediction and intervention (preventive) technologies to help prevent dangerous situations and, again, to raise alarms (for example, falls predictors, monitors for assessing physiological symptoms, room occupancy monitors).

Source: From Beech and Roberts, 2008: 2

There is evidence to suggest that assistive technology devices offer substantial benefits for older people, carers and organisations across health, social care and housing (CSIP, 2006). However, it is also true that the high cost and limited availability of some devices means that provision is far from equitable. While these new technologies have many potential benefits for older people, especially those who are housebound, it is important to ensure that they are implemented in ways that support continued engagement with the community. For example, while new forms of communication such as video linking are convenient ways for formal and informal carers to keep an eye on older people in their own homes, they cannot replace face-to-face contact.

One of the most interesting developments in technology in recent years has been the meteoric rise in popularity of communities that operate via the internet. These are known by a variety of terms, including e-communities, virtual communities and online communities. They have been defined as 'groups of people with common interests that communicate regularly, and for some duration, in an organised way over the internet' (Ridings et al, 2002: 273). These virtual communities can take various forms, including chat rooms, discussion forums, blogs and collaborative websites or 'wikis'. These elements are provided in a range of combinations through social networking websites, including Facebook, MySpace, Friends Reunited and Flickr. High levels of social interaction take place in these online communities (Scott and Johnson, 2005) and their popularity is staggering. For example, in August 2007 the Facebook website had 6.5 million visitors and was used by one in five Britons, with internet access for an average of 5 hours 29 minutes a month. The power of virtual communities in terms of collective activity is considerable, as demonstrated by the 100,000 people who joined an online campaign in less than a week in response to the Burma pro-democracy protests in 2007.

Online networks are often seen as a challenge to traditional concepts of community because they are completely independent of physical place. However, they also share a number of key characteristics. For example, 'real-world' communities are based on common norms of trust and reciprocity while online communities have developed a 'netiquette', with similar principles of reciprocity and support. In the case of online communities this support is often in the form of information rather than physical action. Rheingold (1993a) has argued that online systems of support are particularly powerful because, unlike in the physical world, a single act of helping online can be immediately evident to everyone in that community. Another aspect of online communities that differentiates them from face-to-face ones, and one that often raises concerns, is the issue of personal identity. Internet users can take on any gender, age or personality they choose, a feature that has led to widespread concerns about a range of criminal activities. However, online communities do have systems in place to tackle this. For example, most require that regular users become members, often with greater access and privileges than non-members. In addition, a key feature of membership to many communities is comprehensive profiling and the use of reputation systems to develop trust and build personal connections. These technologies mirror face-to-face communities by providing de facto systems of community governance (Shirky, 1995). Some of these systems include measures of social capital, such as databases that allow users and site managers to monitor and evaluate each member's community participation, leading to scores that measure each individual's reputation within the online community. In many respects, online communities distinguish between members and non-members just as offline ones do.

It would seem, then, that online communities share many characteristics with face-to-face ones. The most obvious difference is that they are not place based, but even this has been challenged by some writers, who suggest that virtual communities are 'real' because participants believe them to be real (for example Harasim, 1993). This analysis sees the internet as a place that people experience as a venue for social interaction and visit in the same way that they might go to a pub or a shopping centre to meet friends. Such views are supported by the importance that networking sites have in the lives of large numbers of young people. For example, one regular user of the Facebook website was reported as saying, 'If I go a day without logging on I feel like I'm missing out, as if I've stayed in on a Friday night'.[1] Online social networking has now evolved into entire virtual worlds, where users are able to interact with each other by manipulating representations of themselves, sometimes know as avatars. In one such world, Second Life (www.secondlife.com), users can explore the environment, meet other residents, socialise, participate in individual and group activities, and even create and buy items and services using virtual money.

While access to an increasing range of information, services and social networks is now available via the internet, it is important to bear in mind that computer use and internet access are relatively low among older age groups. This is largely because only 28% of people over the age of 65 have home internet access, compared with a UK average of 57% of households. Internet use has risen among older people in the past 10 years, but the group still lags behind other age groups (Katz et al, 2001). As few as one in five over-65s have ever used the internet, a figure that is only increasing by a small percentage every year. Similarly, while about 90% of the richest quintile in the 52–59 age group own a computer, compared to 48% of the poorest, this figure falls to 41% and 8% respectively among the 75s and over. These statistics suggest that the current generation of older people remain very much dependent on community-based services and networks. However, more than two thirds of pensioners who are currently not connected say that they would get online if they had the right support; use among those older people with access is relatively high and increasing.

This use is reflected in the emergence of social networking sites aimed at older people. In the US these include Eons (www.eons.com), marketed as 'your online gathering place for people lovin' life on the flip side of 50!', and Boomj (www.boomj.com), providing a 'lifestyle and social network for baby boomers'. One of the first such sites, for older people in the UK was Saga Zone (www.sagazone.co.uk), which opened in 2007 with the aim of providing 'an online community where you create a whole new social network of friends and easily stay in touch from the comfort of your home'. These sites have a relatively simple layout, reflecting a belief that older people are less 'web-savvy' than younger users. However, this is now changing and there is a recognition that by the time they reach retirement age the baby boomer generation will be experienced users of computer technology, largely as a result of skills gained in the workplace.

It seems likely that involvement in online communities will be an increasingly important form of social interaction for older people in the future, but what does this mean for their levels of face-to-face contact? Despite initial assumptions that, because spending time on the internet inevitably reduces opportunities for place-based social interaction, it must lead to reduced 'real-life' community involvement, the evidence suggests that virtual communities may actually augment face-to-face ones. One recent study found that much online contact is between people who see each other and live locally (Wellman and Gulia, 1999). Blanchard and Horan (1998) identify two types of virtual community. In the first category are physically based communities that add electronic resources for their citizens to use. These are town or city websites such as the Blacksburg Electronic Village (www.bev.net/), which was created in 1993 with the aim of developing an online community to link the entire town. The second type are virtual communities of interest, with geographically dispersed members who participate because of their shared interests rather than a shared location. There is a strong argument that both these types of virtual community increase face-to-face interaction, one by connecting physically separate people quickly and easily in ways that often lead to face-to-face relationships (for example, online dating websites often lead to real-world relationships), and the other by providing additional means of communication for residents of local communities. The leads to the conclusion that we must support older people in their use of the internet in order to boost their levels of both virtual and face-to-face social interaction.

8.4 The future of housing with care settings as communities

One crucial issue for this book in the context of the changes that have been outlined so far in this chapter concerns the potential of housing with care settings to operate as communities for older people. In many ways, these forms of housing offer a positive response to the challenges that social changes can present for older people in terms of maintaining community engagement. Retirement villages and extra care housing often include many of the services and facilities that are being closed down in the wider community. This is particularly the case for the larger schemes, and even the smaller ones have had some success in making shops and restaurants economically viable by opening them up to people in the local area. Similarly, many of the challenges in terms of accessibility that the built environment poses for older people in general are addressed in housing with care settings because they are specifically designed to be future proofed and age friendly.

To a large extent it is these features that make specialist retirement housing attractive to many older people compared with general housing, and for this reason it is easy to see them becoming even more popular in the coming years, with demand being fuelled by a shortage of mainstream housing for an ageing population. This view is supported by evidence from several countries to suggest a strong preference among adults to remain in their own homes when they retire rather than moving to any form of institutional care. Findings from a Welsh study suggested that people aged 50 or over were unwilling or unable to think of something that might trigger such a move, be it related to their own health or the condition of their housing (Burholt and Windle, 2004). A similar study in the US found that the majority of people wanted to live independently in their own home on retiring, with an adult retirement community being the second most popular option. While it seems likely that governments will continue policies that support older people in their homes in the wider community rather than providing more specialist provision, there will always be a significant minority of older people who either cannot be supported in mainstream housing or who choose to move into a different type of housing. This is often because they no longer feel safe where they are, they feel their needs are not being met, or they are tempted by the 'community' lifestyle that such alternatives appear to offer.

A belief in the continuing role of specialist retirement housing is reflected in planning guidelines that promote the implementation of local criteria-based policies to address the needs of an ageing population. These include recognising the fact that older people have different needs and increasing the range of appropriate residential accommodation such as retirement villages. There is also an emphasis on addressing sustainability issues, including the relationship of proposed developments to public transport provision and local services and facilities. At the same time there may be pressures that delay the spread of housing with care schemes. In the UK, extra care housing continues to receive considerable government support and subsidy and is often built on brownfield sites, as redevelopment of sheltered housing and care homes, or on the site of outdated health care facilities. The majority of schemes built so far have depended on an element of financial support from the government, which provided grants worth £147 million between 2004 and 2008. A further tranche of funding was announced for 2008/09 but it remains to be seen whether this level of support continues and, if not, whether extra care housing will remain financially viable without it.

The new-style retirement village sector is still at a relatively early stage of development in the UK, particularly in comparison with the US, Australia and New Zealand. However, the sector has grown rapidly in recent years, with villages of ever-increasing size being announced almost every day. Demand for places is high, and many schemes have long waiting lists. However, the limited availability of suitable tracts of land and stringent planning restrictions are major challenges to the development of this sector and are likely to remain so. In the US, Haas and Serow (2002) suggest that while retirement communities will continue to offer a later life environment for a small but significant number of North Americans, a range of government and political processes, such as tax law changes, are likely to reduce their current rate of growth. They also point out that the baby boomer generation is far from homogeneous and some older people are likely to be attracted to a range of new models of retirement housing that will emerge in competition to retirement villages. Retirement schemes targeted at gay and lesbian couples are one example of such a model, although so far these are still based on the standard retirement village format. Another example is co-housing communities, in which residents have a much greater level of control and decision making. Haas and Serow conclude that the amenity-based retirement developments epitomised by the huge golf-centred villages in the US will only be a preferred option for a small number of relatively affluent older people in the future.

As discussed in Chapter Four, housing with care has evolved rapidly in recent decades and is likely to continue to do so, largely in response to changing aspirations, values and views about lifestyle and community involvement. In the UK new models of extra care housing are unveiled every week and many of these aim to improve integration of schemes with local communities. One such trend is the development of schemes that provide services for both residents and those living in the wider community. This started with facilities such as shops and restaurants, but recent advances have seen schemes that incorporate comprehensive community health care facilities. One example is Barton Mews in Staffordshire (see Case Study Thirteen), where a private developer has built a community hospital on the ground floor, with extra care housing apartments on two floors above. All initial costs have been met by the developers, who derive income from a range of sources, including payment per bed from the primary care trust (PCT), rental for use of space by the health authority and a general practice, and sales and service charges generated from the extra care housing. This is an attractive model for the PCT because it significantly reduces their development costs. It also has a number of advantages in terms of promoting community engagement for residents of the extra care apartments. In particular, the fact that the scheme is a redevelopment of a site that is in the heart of an existing village community means that residents have good access to a wide range of services and social networks.

Case Study Thirteen: Barton Mews, Staffordshire, England

Background

Barton Mews in Staffordshire, England, is a private development in partnership with a PCT that provides extra care housing and a range of community health services within a single building. This new build provides three distinct services: extra care housing, an intermediate care service and a GP surgery. The complex was privately funded and income is generated from a range of sources, including payment per bed from the PCT, rental for use of space by the health authority and a general practice, and sales and service charges generated from the extra care housing.

Photo 5: Barton Mews Community Hospital and extra care housing

Housing and care

Retirement accommodation is provided on the first and second floors in 29 one- and two-bedroom apartments, arranged around a rectangular corridor. Facilities include communal lounges, a sun terrace and a reception where residents can order services and pay their weekly bills. Apartments are offered for sale to anyone aged 55 or over on a 125-year lease. A range of care and support services can be purchased by residents in their own apartments 24 hours a day. The philosophy of the scheme is to support independence, and any residents requiring more intensive treatment can use the short-term medical rehabilitation services in the ground floor intermediate care unit. This unit comprises a range of short-stay inpatient beds for intermediate and palliative care along with a unit for the younger physically disabled. These services are provided by the developer under a 30-year contract with the PCT. The ground floor also houses a range of other community health care staff providing health visiting, chiropody, physiotherapy, occupational therapy and speech and language therapy. A local general practice rents part of the ground floor on a 20-year contract.

Learning points

This scheme demonstrates an emerging model of extra care housing that is innovative in terms of integration with community-based health care services. It provides residents and the local community with good access to a wide range of health care facilities.

- The financial model is also innovative. It is attractive to PCTs because it allows for the development of modern community health care facilities without the need for large-scale capital investment. For the private developer, the viability of the scheme depends on income from the sale of extra care apartments.
- The physical layout of the scheme, with extra care accommodation arranged above the health care facilities, makes maximum use of available floor space. This can raise the issue of building height in a residential area and requires careful and imaginative design in order to minimise the impact and blend in with local architecture.
- Combining housing and care with health care services allows for a range of economies of scale. For example, in this development catering, laundry and other 'hotel' services are available to service users, visitors and staff across extra care housing, intermediate care services and a GP surgery.

Source: This case study was initially commissioned by the Housing Learning and Improvement Network and can be found on their website at http://networks.csip.org. uk/IndependentLivingChoices/Housing/, along with a extensive range of resources in relation to housing with care.

Another recent change is the emergence of 'green' retirement villages. For example, some developers in the US are building retirement housing under an agreement that requires participating companies to sign a pledge to reduce their carbon emissions. This involves implementing a range of measures, including solar hot water heating systems, the use of bio-diesel, energy-efficient lighting and recycling programmes. On a similar environmental theme, Highland Green in Maine, a 650-acre (260-hectare) active adult resort community, markets itself as an 'anti-sprawl' community that values community and preservation.[2] In this scheme 230 acres (92 hectares) have been designated as a conservation area that is protected from development and offers hiking trails to residents and people living nearby. Such schemes are the logical continuation of a longstanding strategy of developing niche markets targeted at older people who share similar lifestyle aspirations. Where leisure activities such as golf used to be the mutual obsession that drew residents to many US retirement villages, the desire to be part of a sustainable environment is now being offered as the shared passion that binds together these communities of interest in later life. Another glimpse of a possible way forward for housing with care is the development of NORCs, a concept that is spreading rapidly in the US. For a yearly membership fee older residents in a defined geographical region can access a range of services from volunteers and service providers, including information, household services, transport, shopping, social activities, concierge services and home visits.

These are just a few examples that demonstrate the continuing popularity of housing with care settings for older people and the ways in which they are evolving in order to meet changing perceptions and aspirations for community living. However, they do raise questions about the sustainability of such developments as communities. Both extra care housing and new-style retirement villages are relatively new forms of provision and this, along with the trend towards moving in at an ever-younger age, means that many residents are still healthy and mobile. As a result they are more able to overcome the challenges to getting out and about that are presented by the location of many schemes. This is particularly true for retirement villages, most of which are disconnected from their nearest communities by distance or geography, and where a majority of residents still have their own cars. As a result they are able to access services, facilities and social networks in the wider community. However, this raises concerns about what will happen to their quality of life when their health deteriorates and it becomes more difficult to go beyond the boundaries of the scheme in which they live. Many extra care schemes, in comparison, are embedded within existing neighbourhoods and are better placed to offer possibilities in terms of community engagement for residents as they age. That is not to say that residents cannot become isolated even in these settings and I have presented evidence throughout this book to emphasise the importance of a range of factors in promoting interaction, especially the design of the built environment. However, it is worth noting the recent trend towards larger extra care 'villages'. These are similar to retirement villages in respect of location and size and are therefore likely to face the same challenges in terms of enabling connections with wider communities.

A second area of concern for the sustainability of housing with care settings as communities is the extent to which they offer diversity. This book has taken the view, as explored in Chapter Seven, that diversity is a key element of community. In this context, the relative homogeneity within most retirement villages and extra care housing, particularly in terms of ethnicity, socio-economic status and sexuality, is a major limitation to their success as self-contained communities. It can be argued that these relatively new settings will become more diverse as they evolve and become more common. However, in one respect it is difficult to see how they can become diverse without a complete change in their nature – in terms of their age profile. Retirement villages and extra care housing schemes are age-limited settings, with most having a lower age limit between 50 and 60 years. This feature has been central to their ethos of supporting the specific needs of older people, and their popularity can be seen as a reflection of the failure of a largely youth-focused society to meet these needs. Age segregation also appears to be a key part of their appeal to many – but not all – of those who live in them. This raises major questions for the claims that are often made for these settings as sustainable communities and certainly rules them out of any definition of community that includes diversity and embraces intergenerational relationships.

One interesting aspect of the recent global economic crisis is the possibility that it will alter the nature of retirement housing schemes in order to make them financially viable. For example, many developers are experiencing increasing levels of unsold properties, largely due to the difficulties that potential purchasers are having in selling their existing houses. As a result several retirement villages in the US have been debating whether to scrap age limits as a way of attracting new buyers. In some areas this has already happened, with the residents of the Sun City scheme in Arizona voting to lower the age limit from 55 to 45. However, apart from being a controversial step for some existing residents, this could also affect relations with surrounding areas. For example, retirement villages have often been popular with municipalities because they bring in extra tax revenue while not requiring additional services such as schools. It seems unlikely that financial drivers will lead to the disappearance of age-restricted living altogether, but it will be interesting to see the extent to which retirement settings are forced to reinvent themselves.

8.5 Conclusion

The demographics of an ageing population means that a growing number of people will be in their 'third age', and there is plenty of evidence to suggest that being part of a community becomes increasingly important to us as we grow older. The UK government has recognised the role of sustainable communities in promoting independence and quality of life for older people. For example, 2008 saw the publication of the National Strategy for Housing in an Ageing Society (DCLG, 2008), which promotes the development of neighbourhoods that are age proofed through, among other things, the existence of accessible services and facilities. However, the success of such policies is threatened by a range of social and economic changes that impact on older people's experience of community and the extent to which they are able to engage with community life. Of particular significance is the trend towards the closure of many local services and facilities that have often been the focus of social interaction as well as promoting independence for older people. These include post offices, shops, banks, hospitals and libraries. In the light of such changes, a range of factors need to be addressed in order to maximise the opportunities for older people to maintain a sense of community. Fundamental to this is listening to and acting on older people's views so that service delivery is designed to promote both their independence and their opportunities for community engagement. Achieving this depends on considerable commitment and support from national and local government. One good example of how this can be achieved comes from the Devon Senior Council, which was established in 2008 using grant money awarded by the Department for Work and Pensions. Once established, ongoing funding was provided by Devon County Council and Devon Primary Care Trust. Despite initial scepticism from some older people in the area, membership started to grow and the Senior Council now provides a robust framework for feeding older people's views into decision-making processes. Many statutory agencies now recognise that working in partnership with older people and other service users is a good way to ensure that services are of good quality and cost effective. However, there is still a long way to go. In research carried out by Help the Aged, 54% of older people felt that they were rarely or never asked their opinion on issues affecting them and 33% stated that their local council wasn't good at representing their needs (Help the Aged, 2008a).

There have also been major changes in how technology is used to deliver a range of information and services. This offers many potential advantages for older people in terms of meeting their needs in ways that enhance their health and wellbeing while fitting in with their lifestyles. The use of technology is also seen as a way of delivering personalised care in a cost-effective way. However, these benefits can only be realised if older people are supported to afford and use such technologies, particularly in the context of evidence to suggest that technology use among older people is relatively low. For example, Office for National Statistics figures show that seven in ten over-65s have never used the internet (ONS, 2007). This does not appear to be because older people do not want to make the most of technology. A survey of interactive television services found that older people wanted to access similar services to other age groups, including the internet, games, shopping, email and travel (Boyle et al, 2006). One reason for lower levels of usage is that such technologies are not always designed with older people's needs in mind. For example, only 3% of websites in the European Union fully meet the WC3 web content accessibility guidelines and only 10% achieve a 'limited pass' (Cabinet Office, 2005). There is a danger, therefore, that, while communities and the way we engage with them are changing across many aspects of life, older people will only achieve the many potential benefits of such changes if they are supported in doing so. A range of recent research has started to explore how to improve the accessibility of technology for older people by, for example, devising new methods of cursor use (Hwang et al, 2008) and developing effective and user-friendly reminder systems (Lawson and Nutter, 2008). Innovations such as these are crucial to enable older people to enjoy the enormous benefits of technology, without which they are likely to become increasingly excluded and isolated.

In the context of an ageing population the demand for housing among older people is likely to continue to grow substantially. While the majority will continue to live in general housing in the wider community, it seems likely that demand for housing with care will continue to grow. As long as those older people who can afford to buy into retirement villages see them as the best way of meeting their needs and fulfilling their aspirations, there seems to be no reason why the expansion of this sector should not continue. The future also seems bright for extra care housing, particularly while it continues to receive government support as a way of promoting independence and wellbeing. The extent to which these settings function as communities for their residents remains open to question and depends largely on ensuring good connections with the wider communities in which they sit and promoting intergenerational links. What does seem certain is that older people will wield increasing power as consumers and it will be up to the housing market to provide them with the lifestyle that they demand.

Notes

[1] *Daily Mail*, 26 September 2007.

[2] http://www.highlandgreenmaine.com/

NINE

Conclusion

9.1 Introduction

Retirement housing settings are successful as neighbourhoods designed specifically for older people. They offer age-friendly design and opportunities for social interaction within clear physical boundaries, focusing on similarities and exclusivity rather than diversity and wider integration. The fact that they are specifically age limited contributes to their cohesiveness as neighbourhoods, but it also means that they are not compatible with creating diverse and mixed communities. Ultimately, whether we call them neighbourhoods or communities is immaterial to the people who live in them. All the evidence suggests that a sense of community belonging is important to older people in particular and many of those who move to extra care housing and retirement villages do so for that very reason.

9.2 Community and older people

Community is an intangible concept and therefore extremely difficult to pin down. To a large extent it means different things to different people, shaped by their life histories, experiences and aspirations. At a basic level, community can be defined as a sense of belonging to a social group or groups, based on communalities that span physical space, interests and identities. While early theories of community emphasised the role of place as the focus of social networks and kinship ties, there is agreement in much of the more recent literature that shared interests and identities have supplanted physical place as the main factors in a sense of community, largely as a result of globalisation and increased social mobility. Social networks and social interaction are widely viewed as the 'glue' that binds communities together, as reflected in concepts such as *gemeinschaft* and 'social capital'. The literature identifies three main types of social relationship that vary in terms of physical distance and emotional intensity. These are relationships with close kin, with friends and neighbours and with voluntary and community groups. It has been suggested that having social networks that include all three types of relationship is better than having restricted networks in terms of good health and wellbeing. There has also been a move away from more nostalgic concepts of community that emphasise mutual support in idyllic rural settings towards a recognition that difference, conflict and social exclusion are equally important elements.

In this book I have argued that, while communities have become more complex and fluid, place remains a crucial factor as the venue for social interaction. However, the nature of place in this respect has undoubtedly broadened. Whereas for most people living a hundred years ago social interaction would have centred on the immediate neighbourhood in which they lived, the social networks of today span a much wider geographical area. This is due to a range of factors, including increased social mobility, longer commuting journeys, new communication technologies and globalisation. As a result of social interactions that span larger and multiple physical areas we are likely to be part of several communities, often to varying degrees. We might, for example, feel part of one community where we live, another at work and a third as a result of an interest in a particular leisure activity. Some of our social interactions, be they casual or more organised, continue to take place in and around our residential settings. This is particularly the case for older people, who tend to spend more time in their local neighbourhood than do people from other age groups. This is recognised in the UK government's lifetime neighbourhoods agenda and the World Health Organization's Age-Friendly Cities initiative, both of which emphasise the need for accessible design, age proofing and integration with wider communities.

Within the approach taken by this book – which might be called a theory of 'community in place' – I have put great emphasis on the role of the built environment in promoting social interaction among residents. This is of particular importance to older people, many of whom can benefit greatly from design that enables access to the facilities and public spaces where much social interaction takes place. Conversely, poor design can create barriers to access and reduce such opportunities, leading to isolation and reduced independence. I have also drawn on theories from environmental psychology, sociology and community studies to explore the role of place attachment and a sense of community in supporting quality of life, wellbeing, lifestyle choices and aspirations for older people. There is plenty of evidence to suggest that older people value a sense of community and that it is a major factor in their decisions about where to live. This has been eagerly adopted by both private developers and social landlords, both of whom base much of their promotional literature for housing with care developments on the 'hook line' of community, alongside those of active ageing, peace of mind and security.

Housing quality is an important factor in health and wellbeing for older people. Similarly, the concept of 'home' and attachment to it as a personal place also influence how older people relate to their housing environment in terms of personal identity, social interaction and a sense of control. The emphasis on individual homes in extra care housing and retirement villages may therefore be another key factor in their success. Although length of residence is often linked to the development of place attachment and personal identity, in housing with care settings this is balanced with the feeling of control over their environment that the residents experience. Indeed, it seems likely that this belief in the opportunities to shape their environment in a way that affirms their histories and identities provides one of the main attractions of such settings.

As well as reflecting the appeal of notions of community belonging, the continued popularity of specialist retirement housing is also a symptom of the dissatisfaction that many older people feel with their status and role in modern society. Many older people no longer feel connected to the communities in which they have spent many years, partly due to a failure by society to take into account many of the needs and aspirations of later life. In addition, many older people experience age discrimination in their daily lives, a perception that is supported by a raft of facts and figures (Help the Aged, 2008a). For example:

- 95% of annual travel insurance policies impose an upper age limit;
- people aged 55–64 are twice as likely to be made redundant in organisational restructuring;
- every hour over 50 older people are abused or neglected in their own homes;
- three quarters of NHS clients are aged over 65 but they receive only two fifths of total expenditure.

There is considerable evidence to suggest that continued participation in neighbourhood is important to wellbeing, particularly in later life, and that one of the main effects of poor physical health is reduced social interaction and participation (Allen, 2008). In this book I have also explored a range of social and economic changes and their potential impact on the extent to which older people feel a part of their communities. For example, the trend towards closing a range of local services including post offices, health care facilities, banks and libraries is having a significant effect on older people in particular because of their tendency to depend more on their immediate neighbourhood to meet their needs. Questions about how best to care for growing numbers of older people are now at the forefront of debates about public policy. This urgency is largely driven by predictions that an additional 1.7 million people will have a care and support need by 2028, leading to a potential funding gap of £6 billion. This has resulted in a raft of strategies and plans to overhaul the social care system, which will have major implications for the independence of older people and their opportunities for community participation.

Some of the greatest changes in care delivery in recent years have come in the area of technology. While these developments have many potential benefits for older people, it is important to note that the use of technology among older people is low compared with other age groups. This is particularly significant in terms of the internet, which offers increasing opportunities, not just for accessing services and information but also for social interaction. For example, recent figures suggest that 28% of people aged over 65 have home internet access, compared with 57% of the overall population. It is therefore crucial that older people have appropriate support in using technology through, for example, the development of age-friendly user interfaces.

In addition to this increasing perception among older people that they are being excluded from an ageist society where they feel unsupported and undervalued, many also experience high levels of fear of crime and concerns about young people's anti-social behaviour, often fuelled by alarmist media coverage. Some older people remain in their neighbourhood as they age, maybe out of choice or because they have strong attachment to the area and their local existing social networks. For others it is because they cannot afford to move. As a result, many become isolated and disconnected from the local community, which they find increasingly difficult to access. Growing numbers of older people are moving to specialist retirement housing settings, particularly retirement villages and extra care housing, in search of an environment that does take their needs into account.

9.3 Housing and community in later life

A range of drivers have made the provision of housing for older people a global priority in recent years, particularly the demographics of an ageing population. For example, 76 million North American baby boomers will reach retirement age over the next two decades. In anticipation of increased demand the UK government has announced plans to build 3 million extra homes by 2020 (DCLG, 2007). There is also an emphasis on ensuring that any new housing supports the development of sustainable communities. Indeed, this is one of the core aims of the new UK Homes and Communities Agency, which was established in 2009. This approach was reflected in a strategy for older people (Housing Corporation, 2008) that focused on providing new homes within communities to meet the needs of older people for support, care and self-determination. Although the emphasis of government strategy in many countries is on supporting older people in general housing, there is increasing demand for housing with care. Retirement villages and extra care housing have become particularly popular in this context, largely because they are seen to promote independence, wellbeing and community living for people in their own homes, while at the same time supporting ageing in place through the provision of flexible care packages. They are also age-segregated settings, with most having a minimum age limit of between 50 and 60 years old.

Retirement villages are usually much bigger than extra care housing or assisted living facilities. This is particularly true in the US, where they are largely based on shared leisure interests, particularly golf, and the largest has over 75,000 residents. Extra care villages are smaller and depend on external services to a greater extent. However, their size makes them easier to locate within or near to existing communities. In contrast, retirement villages tend to require much larger sites and as a result many are in relatively isolated rural locations. At the same time, their size brings economies of scale that allow the provision onsite of a greater range of the services and facilities required for daily living. However, their size and location also have implications for the ability of residents to interact with the wider community and maintain contacts with external social networks. This is particularly important in the context of evidence that suggests that opportunities for social interaction are crucial to independence, wellbeing and the development of a sense of community for older people. An important implication for housing with care is that such opportunities need to be not only between residents but also with social networks beyond the scheme.

The size of retirement villages is also a factor in their relationship to the wider community. For example, the residents of one village in Florida outnumber the county residents and have used their voting power to change the basis on which local representatives are elected. At the same time, legal statutes exempt them from contributing funds towards local schools and other community-based services. Many of these larger developments also impose a range of regulations on residents that can restrict their sense of control over the community in which they live.

In the US a range of niche markets are emerging that focus on specific lifestyles and aspirations. These include villages with Christian affiliations, GLBT villages, university-based retirement villages and developments aimed at older people who want to pursue a 'green' lifestyle. In Holland and several Scandinavian countries different models of housing with care have emerged. These tend to be based on principles of diversity within small-scale domestic-type environments. One scheme in Denmark provides family units along side co-housing for older people. There is also much emphasis on promoting intergenerational social interaction.

This book has shown that one of the major attractions of housing with care settings for older people is the perception that they offer the opportunity for them to be part of a community. But can they meet this expectation? To a large extent those who move to housing with care settings are choosing to sacrifice their longstanding place attachments in favour of new environments, in which they believe they will develop a sense of belonging. The success of this form of 'elective belonging' depends largely on their ability to develop rapidly a sense of home and feelings of belonging that affirm each individual's self-identity and life history. In the context of a theory of community in place adopted by this book, these settings provide environments that are specifically designed to meet the needs and aspirations of older people, including those people with physical and cognitive impairments, and to do so within a well-defined physical space. These features support the relatively rapid development of a sense of attachment among residents who have given up the familiarity of their previous residential settings and are eager to adopt the 'lifestyle of belief' (Biggs et al, 2001) that they aspire to. This interpretation complements Brent's (2004) argument that the real essence of 'community' is the very desire for community itself. However, there are individual differences in ability to make and remake place and having a previous experience of doing so may be a key factor. Rowles (1983) has suggested that successful techniques include replicating previous arrangements of furniture, effective psychological preparation, developing social strategies for connecting with new neighbours and the use of artefacts such as family photos. The fact that many achieve this remaking of place is reflected in the high levels of satisfaction found among residents, although it is also important to note that there is also a greater risk of exclusion in these settings for those with higher levels of frailty.

Chapter Six discussed a range of factors that can help promote social interaction in housing with care settings. These include the design of the built environment, the provision of facilities and services, the model of care in operation and having opportunities to take part in social activities. If properly considered and implemented, these factors can help to promote a sense of community and belonging. However, as concluded in Chapter Seven, retirement villages and extra care housing are often very limited in the extent to which they promote and accommodate diversity. Indeed, they are widely marketed on the basis of the homogeneity of residents' aspirations and interests. For example, one developer in the US described how their retirement villages offer the opportunity to be 'part of an active senior living community with like-minded individuals, [where] you can enjoy many social activities and experiences in good company'.[1] Similarly, an extra care housing scheme in England was promoted on the basis of offering 'independence, comfort and security within a community of like-minded people'.[2] This strategy of appealing to older people with similar interests can also be seen in the trend for retirement villages for specific groups, particularly in the US, such as GLBTs, university alumni and 'greens'. This emphasis on a high degree of 'sameness' is reflected in an overall lack of diversity among residents, particularly in terms of ethnicity, socio-economic status and age. This is in stark contrast to an ageing population that is increasingly diverse in terms of cognitive functioning, mobility, health status, care needs, lifestyle and aspirations. It also contradicts UK government policies that view diverse communities as more sustainable and leading to reduced social exclusion (see for example the 2007 Sustainable Communities Act). There have been recent attempts to address this in the UK through the inclusion of mixed tenure and affordable housing in some schemes. Such models are relatively new, and early research findings highlight the complexities of encouraging cross-tenure social interaction and the challenges of creating and managing mixed communities (Evans and Means, 2007).

Perhaps the greatest challenge to diversity in housing with care lies in the fact that these are by their very nature age-segregated settings, with residency usually open to people aged 55 or over. This raises major questions with regard to intergenerational relationships. Two UK charities have suggested that the young and the old have become so estranged and out of touch that there is a need to establish organised opportunities for intergenerational contact in order to promote mutual understanding (4Children, 2008). Their report expresses concerns that the increasing distance between these age groups may lead to social problems unless action is taken to re-establish relationships that are otherwise increasingly marked by fear, ignorance and misunderstanding. There is a strong argument that it is better to promote intergenerational contact by supporting older people in appropriate housing within mainstream society, while at the same time making use of their experiences and skills, rather than creating special environments to meet the needs of older people. This would of course mean paying far more attention to making mainstream society age friendly.

In this book I have argued that diversity is a key element of communities and that, while it is possible to envisage housing with care schemes becoming more diverse in terms of ethnicity and socio-economic status, the fact that their very nature excludes age diversity means that they cannot be considered as communities in any real sense. This is not to say that they are unsuitable environments for older people per se. Throughout this book I have presented examples of the many ways in which extra care housing and retirement communities can promote quality of life, health and wellbeing, particularly thorough appropriate design of the built environment. However, they can be most accurately described as age-friendly neighbourhoods rather than as communities. This is not to deny the importance of neighbourhoods to quality of life for residents, especially in terms of social relationships. Many writers have highlighted the importance of neighbourliness as a manifestation of the health of a social environment. This can bring a range of benefits, including lower anxiety about crime, a clean and attractive environment, and a sense of belonging (see for example Abrams and Bulmer, 1986). Similarly, Campbell (1958) suggested that groups are more cohesive where members pursue a common goal, are interpersonally similar and have shared and stable boundaries. Ashida and Heaney (2008) emphasised the importance of social support for older people and suggested that it is often provided within networks that are large, dense and homogeneous in terms of the demographic characteristics of members. To this extent the relative lack of diversity among residents could, ironically, be seen as an advantage in terms of the development of social ties and connectedness.

If neighbourliness is based on having common interests, common purpose and a common identity, these are all key elements of housing with care settings and as such they can be said to contribute towards success as neighbourhoods. Another common feature of extra care housing and retirement villages is the existence of very clear physical boundaries between them and the surrounding area. This emphasis on spatial segregation reinforces distinctions between self and others and is also integral to perceptions of social difference (Wilton, 1998). This is particularly interesting in the light of the research carried by out by Bernard et al (2007), which found that the perceived benefits of living in a retirement village were partly dependent on comparisons with those who were excluded. It would seem that being physically distinct and separate may also be key to the success of housing with care schemes as neighbourhoods in which residents feel they belong. At the same time, Kearns and Forrest (2000) suggest that cohesive neighbourhoods are not necessarily good things because they can imply exclusion and a majority imposing its value system on a minority.

A number of questions have been asked about the long-term future of housing with care settings. This chapter has already raised concerns about their focus on age segregation and what this means for intergenerational relationships. While there may be ways to encourage residents to mix with younger people through organised activities, and so on, this model of keeping the old and the young apart cannot be desirable or sustainable in the long term. While it may offer those older people who can afford it an environment in which their needs are put first, it can also restrict their opportunities for active involvement in wider communities. A recent UK report identified this as an area in which much more needs to be done, and called on local councils to work with older people to age-proof mainstream services (Audit Commission, 2008). In this respect retirement villages and extra care housing can be contrasted with multigenerational housing schemes in Holland, where the focus is on shared living spaces and interaction between young and old.

Blandy (2008) suggested that gated communities represent a voluntary withdrawal from the wider community. Even without the obvious separation that gating provides, by choosing any specialist, relatively isolated retirement setting, residents have to a large extent opted out of wider society as a lifestyle choice. While this may have short-term advantages in terms of meeting the specific needs of some older people, it is not conducive to a diverse and tolerant society. As Kearns and Forrest (2000: 1001) put it, 'One place's cohesion may be society's deconstruction'. Retirement villages also raise questions of equity between those older people living in purpose-built age-friendly settings and those who choose not to move or who cannot afford to do so. Will the latter become increasingly isolated and excluded as a result of the changes in the neighbourhoods where they have aged in place, over which they feel they have little control? In this scenario there is a danger that retirement villages become enclaves of the privileged.

Another concern focuses on the fact that, while there is a trend towards moving into housing with care schemes at a younger age, the average care needs of residents will inevitably increase as they grow older. Kuhn (1977) suggested that these settings risk becoming ghettoes of increasing dependency, leading to significant implications for the ability of residents to enjoy opportunities for social interaction, both within the scheme and beyond. There are also concerns about the sustainability of the larger retirement villages in the US and elsewhere, and it has been suggested that falling house prices, the ageing population and the increasing costs of care could mean that many become 'ghost towns' (Blechman, 2008). The recent rapid growth in these schemes has been driven largely by the fact that the baby boomer population bulge is now entering retirement, leading to questions about what will happen when they begin to reach the end of their lives and the demands on housing decrease? This is likely to have significant implications, not only for the financial models on which they are based but also for the social lives of those who remain living in the schemes.

While this book has treated retirement villages and extra care housing as similar forms of housing with care, it is important to emphasise some key differences between these two settings that affect the extent to which they can function as communities. While extra care housing schemes are usually smaller than retirement villages and their residents depend on good access to external services and facilities, their size makes them easier to locate within or near to existing communities. In contrast, retirement villages tend to require much larger sites and as a result many are in relatively isolated rural locations. This has implications for the ability of residents to interact with the wider community and maintain contacts with external social networks. At the same time, their larger size brings economies of scale in the form of the provision on site of many of the services and facilities required for daily living.

Despite widespread portrayals of modern societies that are suffering from a lack of community spirit, there is plenty of evidence to suggest that a sense of community remains important, particularly to older people. This is reflected in marketing campaigns that depict extra care housing and retirement villages as 'communities of like-minded people'. The subtext of much of this advertising is an appeal to those who feel alienated by a youth-focused society, which places little value on the experiences and skills of older people. For many older people housing with care settings offer a positive response to the challenges that social changes can present for older people in terms of day-to-day living. For example, they can provide a good range of facilities and ample opportunities for social interaction within a built environment that has been specifically designed for older people. In this book I have argued that the popularity of such settings reflects the fact that new cohorts of retirees entering increasingly long periods of retirement feel that their existing communities do not meet their needs and lifestyle aspirations. It can also be seen as an acknowledgement of societal failure to integrate the young and the old. This book concludes that these settings are more effective as 'healthy' neighbourhoods than as communities, largely because of their lack of diversity; what we choose to call them is essentially irrelevant. Residents have a great deal invested in the success of housing with care settings, both financially and emotionally, and therefore they are communities to the extent that the residents want and believe them to be so.

It seems likely that there will continue to be strong demand for housing with care environments among those older people for whom they are an option. This may be boosted by the increasing assertiveness and spending power of the cohort of baby boomers whose aspirations for retirement include a lifestyle based on a vision of community. While new models are continuing to evolve in response to changing needs and aspirations, the desire to be part of a community seems likely to remain one of the main reasons for such a choice. In contrast, those who do not have the opportunity to move to such environments risk feeling isolated and excluded because of the changes that take place in the neighbourhoods where they have aged in place. One viable alternative strategy is to put more resources into supporting older people to remain connected to their existing communities through a range of measures such as providing housing that is more suitable, placing more emphasis on age-friendly built environments and reversing the closure of local services and facilities on which older people often rely. A good model for this is provided by some of the programmes described in Chapter Five that have been developed in the US to support older people in NORCs. Finally, this book has raised major questions about the extent to which age-segregated models of housing with care are sustainable and the implications for relationships between the young and the old. In contrast, some examples of intergenerational co-housing in Holland and Scandinavia appear to offer a far more positive vision.

Notes

[1] www.actsretirement.com/lifestyle_retirementresortlifestyle.asp

[2] www.extracarehousing.org.uk/housing/details.aspx?lst=andser=4andman=A udley%20Court%20Estates%20Ltdandmanid=5179andsm=6andvm=listandks= 17125andctb=1

Appendix

1: Opening doors to independence: a longitudinal study exploring the contribution of extra care housing to the care and support of older people with dementia

Authors: Sarah Vallelly, Simon Evans, Tina Fear and Robin Means
Published in 2006 by Housing 21, London
Funded by the Housing Corporation and Housing 21

The main aim of this study was to evaluate the contribution that extra care housing can make to the long-term care and support of people with dementia. The longitudinal design incorporated a mixed methodology, combining a quantitative component that tracked 103 people with dementia in extra care housing with an indepth qualitative element that focused on six diverse extra care schemes as case study sites. The case studies involved over 125 interviews with tenants with dementia, their relatives, care staff, other tenants and senior managers from local health and social care partner organisations. In addition, a range of local and regional policies and strategies were analysed in relation to each of the six schemes.

Findings

For the tenants and relatives interviewed in this study, independence was one of the most highly valued aspects of living in extra care housing. Three elements of the extra care environment emerged as particularly important in supporting independence for people with dementia:

• the freedom to come and go within and beyond the housing scheme;
• maximising opportunities to 'do things' for themselves;
• having choices about how to spend their time.

Conclusion

This study demonstrated that independence is one of the most important elements of quality of life for people with dementia living in extra care housing. A range of factors in the physical, social and care environments should be considered in order to maximise independence. Good design of individual apartments and communal areas, the provision of appropriate activities and the availability of flexible care and support were all found to be important. However, the interaction between such factors can be complex. For example, providing social activities can only help encourage social contact if tenants can easily get to such events. For tenants with dementia this requires design that is dementia friendly and accessible and, for some, requires staff being available to escort them. Similarly, electronic assistive technology has considerable potential to promote independence by maximising capabilities and minimising risk. However, to happen effectively, this requires more specialist staff training in the use of such technology, combined with an increased understanding of how to respond to challenging behaviours.

Extra care housing can maximise the opportunities for people with dementia to live independent lives. For example, an 82-year-old man in this study enjoyed daily walks within the local area and beyond, including occasional visits to the local bookmakers. To create an environment that allows such opportunities for independence requires well-developed policies, strategies and practices that take into account a wide range of factors in a holistic and person-centred way.

2: Balanced retirement communities? A case study of Westbury Fields

Authors: Simon Evans and Robin Means
Published in 2007 by the St Monica Trust, Bristol, www.stmonicatrust.org.uk/publications.asp
Funded by the St Monica Trust

The overall aim of the study was to explore the extent to which residents with a wide range of housing and care histories and from different socio-economic backgrounds can be integrated into a single retirement community. Specific research objectives included developing a profile of residents in terms of their backgrounds and dependency levels prior to moving to Westbury Fields, exploring social networks within and beyond the village, and examining the impact of social background and dependency levels on interaction between residents. Research methods included indepth interviews with 37 residents and eight staff, a housing questionnaire to 34 residents and the use of routinely collected data to profile the living arrangements and health/social care needs of residents.

The village featured in this study aimed to attract a diverse population from different socio-economic backgrounds by means of its various housing tenures and care options: the target residents ranged from active, independent people to those requiring a high degree of care and support. The village accommodated over 200 older people who occupied privately owned retirement apartments, a nursing care home and an extra care housing facility. The village was a gated development in a residential suburb of a large city that straddles two distinct neighbourhoods. The development was also within walking distance of a long-established village with many shops, a library, restaurants and other amenities. Both entrances to the landscaped site had security gates and a surveillance system and the site staff included 24-hour security personnel. Onsite facilities included a gym with spa pool, a croquet court, a library, carpet bowls, a residents' lounge/dining room, two computer rooms, two hairdressing salons, a pub and two restaurants.

Summary of findings

Overall, residents reported high levels of satisfaction with the village. Four aspects of life at Westbury Fields were particularly important: independence; choice; the role of the staff; and the philosophy of care. Staff experiences of working at Westbury Fields were also positive, with great value being attributed to team working and quality of care. A range of factors were highlighted by residents as important to maximising independence. These included flexible care and support; the role of staff; the existence of good facilities; the provision of a range of social activities; the location of the village; the availability of transport; feeling safe; and financial security. Residents expressed mixed views concerning the extent to which Westbury Fields worked as a community. There was evidence that a number of neighbourhoods had developed within the village, corresponding to the different types of housing. Many residents and staff felt that it was early days for the village in terms of being a community but that things were slowly moving in that direction.

The research identified four key factors that affected the process of the development of a community: the physical design, the social experience, quality of life and independence, and the philosophy of care. Most residents embraced the concept of mixed tenure and dependency within the village, but for a minority such diversity was a barrier to the development of a community.

Conclusions

- Westbury Fields is an imaginative attempt to offer housing options within a retirement village that incorporates a wide range of residents with different health/social care needs and socio-economic backgrounds.
- Maximising the independence of residents is central to promoting choice, quality of life and development of a community. A range of factors are important to this process, including design and location, quality and philosophy of care, support and staff, the range of facilities and activities and good operational practice.
- Careful attention to village layout can promote social interaction, particularly for residents with impaired mobility. In addition, the accessibility of comfortable communal areas is crucial to the development of social networks.
- The location within the village of a wide range of facilities and activities encourages shared ownership and access by residents.
- The good design of buildings and individual apartments can maximise accessibility and independence for all residents within a community.
- Careful consideration needs to be given to the impact of phased opening of accommodation on community development.
- While it is recognised that some residents appreciate the security that gates and fences provide, these can also be perceived as a barrier, particularly in relation to interfaces with the wider community.

- Facilitating residents in accessing social networks and services in the wider community requires careful consideration. The provision of appropriate transport appears to be of particular importance.
- Residents value care provision that is flexible, person centred and inclusive, provided by well-trained and fully supported staff. This can enable them to maintain their independence and interact with the community.

Westbury Fields retirement village illustrates the ways in which a number of these factors affect the development of a 'balanced' community. For example, the location and layout of the village on a level site within established local communities promotes broad social integration and inclusion; the provision of a wide range of accessible facilities and activities, including a pub, a restaurant, a gym, communal lounges and computer rooms, supports independence and social networking.

3: Promoting social well-being in extra care housing

Authors: Simon Evans and Sarah Vallelly
Published in 2007 by the Joseph Rowntree Foundation, York, www.jrf.org.uk/knowledge/findings/socialcare/2115.asp
Funded by the Joseph Rowntree Foundation

The overall aim of this study was to explore the social wellbeing of 'frail' people living in extra care housing. Data were collected through 36 indepth interviews with extra care residents and managers from six extra care housing schemes in England. In selecting tenants as potential research participants, managers were asked to aim for diversity in terms of three criteria: extent of physical frailty, age and the 'localness' of tenants.

Findings

Interviews with tenants and scheme managers identified a range of factors that played a part in promoting social wellbeing for people living in extra care housing. The following emerged as particularly important themes:

- *Friendship and social interaction:* for many tenants, the friendships and acquaintances that they developed within the scheme were the basis of their social lives. Opportunities for social interaction focused on a range of organised social activities. For others, the ability to maintain social networks in the wider community was equally important.
- *The role of family carers:* family members played a large part in the lives of many tenants in terms of the practical and emotional support they offered. Many of the tenants interviewed during this study had family living locally but, even for some tenants whose family lived further away, they were an important source of social contact.

- *Engaging with the wider community:* tenants who took part in the study engaged with a range of amenities in the local community, and local community members accessed resources within the housing scheme. There was a real sense that being part of community activities that took place away from the housing scheme made life more interesting, stimulating, exciting and engaging.
- *The role of facilities:* the extra care housing schemes that took part in this project had a range of onsite facilities available. These included shops, restaurants, communal areas, hairdressers, beauty salons, gardens, day centres and guest rooms. For many tenants, such facilities served as important venues for social interaction and were at the core of their social lives.
- *Design, location and layout:* a common design feature of the schemes in this study was an indoor 'street', a central route through the scheme, around which a range of facilities are arranged. If sensitively designed, this can provide a safe, dry and level environment that maximises accessibility and increases the opportunity for tenants to meet each other for both formal and informal social activities. The positioning of schemes in rural locations presents particular challenges in terms of enabling tenants to engage with the local community.
- *Staffing issues and the culture of care:* to a large extent, the overall approach within any scheme towards tenant welfare and wellbeing is determined by the policies of provider organisations and the experience and attitude of scheme managers and other staff. A person-centred approach to care provision supports social wellbeing through key-worker systems, along with a flexible approach to spending time with tenants.

Conclusions

This research explored the social lives of people living in extra care housing and identified a range of factors that can impact on their social wellbeing. Most participants reported a high level of satisfaction with their social wellbeing and overall quality of life. Having their own home and the independence that it provided seemed to be an important part of this, as was the overall extra care housing environment, the friends they made within it and the contact that they had with the wider community. A minority of participants were less integrated socially and reported feeling isolated and lonely at times. This was most common among specific groups of tenants, including people with physical frailties or impaired mobility, people with cognitive impairment and single men.

Implications for practice

- The social wellbeing of tenants is an important factor that needs to be taken into account fully in the planning, design and management of extra care housing.
- It is important to provide and facilitate activities that are adequately funded and cater for a range of interests and abilities. Good practice could be standardised

through the specification of activity requirements in contracts with local authorities.

- The opportunity to develop and maintain a social life that is independent of the housing scheme is crucial. This means facilitating tenants to engage with the wider community through, for example, accessible design and affordable transport.
- There is a need for an evidence base of good practice for supporting social wellbeing. The involvement of designers, local planners, service providers and other interested parties at an early stage of development is crucial to achieving schemes that are integrated with the local community.
- Restaurants and shops are important as venues for social interaction and should be considered in the core specifications when commissioning a scheme.
- Some tenants are at particular risk of social exclusion, including people who have recently moved in, people who do not receive regular contact from family or friends and people who have impaired mobility. Tenants likely to come into these categories should be identified and offered appropriate additional support.
- A person-centred approach to care provision can contribute towards social wellbeing. This should be based on comprehensive personal profiles developed in collaboration with tenants, their relatives and referrers.
- Key-worker systems can maximise the benefits of interaction with staff, particularly for tenants at the greatest risk of social exclusion. Staff need appropriate training and support to enable them to promote social wellbeing.
- Diversity is a key feature of extra care housing in terms of age, care needs, health status, cognitive functioning and aspirations. Social wellbeing depends on a range of stakeholders understanding and tolerating this diversity, including tenants, family carers and professionals across housing, health and social care. Clear information and good communication are key to achieving this.
- It is important that care and support services are provided and maintained outside core hours of work. In addition to ensuring that sufficient paid staff are available at these times, a number of creative solutions have been indicated in this study, such as engaging volunteers and local people with a connection to the scheme to provide activities.
- The findings of this report suggest the need for information on supporting social wellbeing to be included in profiles of extra care housing and other long-term care options.
- Extra care housing is well-placed to deliver the strategic objectives outlined in *Opportunity age* (DWP, 2005) of promoting wellbeing and the health of older people in the communities it serves. More research is needed to explore the impact that extra care has within the wider community.

References

4Children, 2008. 'For all ages: bringing different generations closer together, London: 4 Children/Counsel and Care, at www.4children.org.uk/information/show/ref/1411

Abrams, P. and Bulmer, M., 1986. *Neighbours: the work of Philip Abrams*, Cambridge: Cambridge University Press.

Aldridge, F. and Tuckett, A., 2007. *The road to nowhere? The NIACE survey on adult participation in learning*, London: NIACE.

Allen, J., 2008. *Older people and wellbeing*, London: Institute for Public Policy Research.

Anderson, B.R.O.G., 1991. *Imagined communities: reflections on the origin and spread of nationalism*, London: Verso.

Antonucci, T.C., Akiyama, H. and Lansford, J.E., 1998. 'Negative effects of close social relations', *Family Relations*, **47**(4), pp 379–84.

Ashida, S. and Heaney, C.A., 2008. 'Differential associations of social support and social connectedness with structural features of social networks and the health status of older adults', *Journal of Aging and Health*, **20**(7), pp 872-93.

Askham, J. and Hancock, R., 1999. *To have and to hold: the bond between older people and the homes they own*, York: for the Joseph Rowntree Foundation by York Publishing Services.

Atchley, R.C., 1998. 'Activity adaptations to the development of functional limitations and results for subjective well-being in later adulthood: a qualitative analysis of longitudinal panel data over a 16-year period', *Journal of Aging Studies*, **12**(1), pp 19–38.

Atkinson, R., 2003. 'Addressing urban social exclusion through community involvement in urban regeneration', in R. Imrie and M. Raco (eds), *Urban renaissance? New Labour, community and urban policy*, Bristol: The Policy Press, pp 101–20.

Atkinson, R. and Kintrea, K., 2000. 'Owner-occupation, social mix and neighbourhood impacts', *Policy and Politics*, **28**(1), pp 93–108.

Attwood, C., Singh, G. and Prime, D., 2003. *2001 Home Office citizenship survey: people, families and communities*, London: Home Office Research, Development and Statistics Directorate.

Audit Commission, 2008. *Don't stop me now. Preparing for an ageing population*, London: Trident Publishing.

Bartlett, J. and Leadbeater, C., 2008. *Making it personal*, London: Demos.

Bauman, Z., 2001. *Community: seeking safety in an insecure world*, Cambridge: Polity.

Beck, U., 2000. *What is globalization?*, Cambridge: Polity.

Beech, R. and Roberts, D., 2008. *SCIE research briefing 28: assistive technology and older people*, London: SCIE.

Berkman, L.F., Glass, T., Brissette, I. and Seeman, T.E., 2000. 'From social integration to health: Durkheim in the new millennium', *Social Science and Medicine*, **51**(6), pp 843–57.

Bernard, M., 2008. 'Sustainable futures and the development of new retirement villages', presentation at the Annual Conference of the British Society of Gerontology, 2008, atwww.keele.ac.uk/research/lcs/csg/downloads/index.htm#Other

Bernard, M., Bartlam, B., Biggs, S. and Sim, J., 2004. *New lifestyles in old age: health, identity and well-being in Berryhill retirement village*, Bristol: The Policy Press.

Bernard, M., Bartlam, B., Sim, J. and Biggs, S., 2007. 'Housing and care for older people: life in an English purpose built retirement village', *Ageing and Society*, **27**(4), pp 555–78.

Biggs, S., Bernard, M., Kingston, P. and Nettleton, H., 2001. 'Lifestyles of belief: narrative and culture in a retirement community', *Ageing and Society*, **20**(6), pp 649–72.

Blakely, E.J. and Snyder, M.G., 1999. *Fortress America: gated communities in the United States*, Washington: Brookings Institute Press.

Blanchard, A. and Horan, T., 1998. 'Virtual communities and social capital', *Social Science Computer Review*, **16**(3), pp 293-307.

Blandy, S., 2008. 'Secession or cohesion? Exploring the impact of gated communities', in J. Flint and D. Robinson (eds), *Community cohesion in crisis? New dimensions of diversity and difference*, Bristol: The Policy Press, pp 239–57.

Blandy, S., Lister, D., Atkinson, R. and Flint, J., 2003. 'Gated communities: a systematic review of the evidence', ESRC Centre for Neighbourhood Research, at www.neighbourhoodcentre.org.uk

Blazer, D.G., 2003. 'Depression in late life: review and commentary', *Journals of Gerontology Series A: Biological Sciences and Medical Sciences*, **58**(3), pp 249–65.

Blechman, A., 2008. *Leisureville: adventures in America's retirement utopias*, Boston: Atlantic Monthly Press.

Bourdieu, P., 1986. 'The forms of capital', in J. Richardson (ed), *Handbook of theory and research for the sociology of education*, New York: Greenwood, pp 241–58.

Bowling, A., 1997. *Measuring health: a review of quality of life measurement scales*, Milton Keynes: Open University Press.

Boyle, H., Nicolle, C., Maguire, M. and Mitchell, V., 2006. 'Older users' requirements for interactive television', in J. Clarkson, P. Langdon and P. Robinson (eds) *Designing Accessible Technology*, London: Springer, pp 85–92.

Brent, J., 1997. 'Community without unity', in P. Hoggett (ed), *Contested communities: experiences, struggles, policies*, Bristol: The Policy Press, pp 68–83.

Brent, J., 2004. 'The desire for community: illusion, confusion and paradox', *Community Development Journal*, **39**(3), pp 213–23.

Brenton, M., 2005. 'Supporting diversity in Tower Hamlets', Case Study 7, Housing LIN, London: Care Services Improvement Partnership, at http://www.dhcarenetworks.org.uk/_library/Resources/Housing/Practice_examples/Supporting_Diversity_in_Tower_Hamlet_January_2005_pdf_-_124Kb.pdf

Brown, S., 1995. 'Crime and safety in whose "community"? Age, everyday life, and problems for youth policy', *Youth and Policy*, **48**, pp 27–48.

Burholt, V. and Windle, G., 2004. 'Future housing for older people', *Working with Older People*, **8**(3), pp 31–4.

Burnett, J., 2007. 'Britain's "civilising project": community cohesion and core values', *Policy and Politics*, **35**(2), pp 353–7.

Cabinet Office, 2005. *E-accessibility of public sector services in the European Union*, London: HMSO.

Cahill, S. and South, K., 2002. 'Policy issues affecting lesbian, gay, bisexual, and transgender people in retirement', *Generations*, **26**(2), pp 49–54.

Calhoun, C.J., 1980. 'Community: toward a variable conceptualization for comparative research', *Social History*, **5**(1), pp 105–29.

Campbell, D.T., 1958. 'Common fate, similarity and other indices of the status of aggregates of persons as social entities', *Behavioural Science*, **3**(1), pp 14–25.

Carvel, J., 2007. 'Prospect of moving to a care home frightens two thirds of Britons', *The Guardian*, 3 December, at www.guardian.co.uk/society/2007/dec/03/longtermcare

Chalfont, G., 2005. 'Creating enabling outdoor environments for residents', *Nursing and Residential Care*, **7**(10), pp 454–7.

Cheshire, P., 2007. *Are mixed communities the answer to segregation and poverty?*, York: Joseph Rowntree Foundation.

Clough, R., Leamy, M., Miller, V. and Bright, L., 2004. *Housing decisions in later life*, Basingstoke: Palgrave Macmillan.

Cohen, A.P., 1985. *The symbolic construction of community*, London: Routledge.

Colclough, G. and Sitaraman, B., 2005. 'Community and social capital: what is the difference?', *Sociological Enquiry*, **75**(4), pp 474–96.

Colker, D., 2007. 'Gay seniors cherish enclave', *Colorado Springs Gazette*, 7 November.

Croucher, K., 2008. *Housing choices and aspirations of older people*, London: HMSO.

Croucher, K., Hicks, L. and Jackson, K., 2006. *Housing with care for later life: a literature review*, York: Joseph Rowntree Foundation.

Croucher, K., Please, N. and Bevan, M., 2003. *Living at Hartrigg Oaks: residents' views of the UK's first continuing care retirement community*, York: Joseph Rowntree Foundation.

Crow, G. and Allan, G., 1994. *Community life: an introduction to local social relations*, Hemel Hempstead: Harvester Wheatsheaf.

CSIP (Care Services Improvement Partnership), 2006. *Building an evidence base for successful telecare implementation. Updated report of the evidence working group of the Telecare Policy Collaborative*, London: Department of Health.

Dalley, G., 2002. 'Independence and autonomy: the twin peaks of ideology', in K. Sumner (ed), *Our homes, our lives. Choice in later life living arrangements*, London: Centre for Policy on Ageing, pp 10–35.

Darton, R., Baumker, T., Callaghan, L., Holder, J., Netten, A. and Towers, A., 2008. 'Evaluation of the extra care housing funding initiative: initial report', PSSRU Discussion Paper 2506/2, Personal Social Services Research Unit, University of Kent, Canterbury.

Daum, M., 1982. 'Preference for age-homogeneous versus age-heterogeneous social integration', *Journal of Gerontological Social Work*, **4**(3&4), pp 41-55.

Davies, W.K.D. and Herbert, D. 1993. *Communities within cities: an urban social geography*, London: Belhaven Press.

DCLG (Department for Communities and Local Government), 2006. *Strong and prosperous communities*, London: The Stationery Office.

DCLG, 2007. *Homes for the future: more affordable, more sustainable*, London: The Stationery Office.

DCLG, 2008. *Lifetime homes, lifetime neighbourhoods: a national strategy for housing in an ageing society*, London: The Stationery Office.

Department of Health, 2001. *National service framework for older people*, London: The Stationery Office.

Department of Health, 2002. *The health survey for England: the health of older people*, London: The Stationery Office.

Department of Health, 2009. *Living well with dementia: a national dementia strategy*, London: The Stationery Office.

Department for Transport, 2005. *Transport statistics bulletin: national travel survey 2005*, London: The Stationery Office.

Despres, C., 1991. 'The meaning of home: literature review and directions for future research and theoretical development', *Journal of Architectural and Planning Research*, **8**(2), pp 96–115.

Durkheim, E., 1951. *Suicide, a study in sociology*, New York: The Free Press.

Durkheim, E., 1964. *The rules of the sociological method*, New York: The Free Press.

DWP (Department for Work and Pensions), 2005. *Opportunity age: meeting the challenges of ageing in the 21st century*, London: The Stationery Office.

EAC (Elderly Accommodation Counsel), 2008a. *Statistics on housing with care in England*, London: Elderly Accommodation Counsel.

EAC, 2008b. *Guide to retirement villages in the UK*, London: EAC.

Eales, J., Keefe, J. and Keating, N., 2008. 'Age friendly rural communities', in N. Keating (ed), *Rural ageing: a good place to grow old?*, Bristol: The Policy Press, pp 109–20.

Edwards, C., 2003. 'Disability and the discourses of the Single Regeneration Budget', in R. Imrie and M. Raco (eds), *Urban renaissance? New Labour, community and urban policy*, Bristol: The Policy Press, pp 163–80.

Eshelman, P.E. and Evans, G.W., 2002. 'Home again: environmental predictors of place attachment and self-esteem for new retirement community residents', *Journal of Interior Design*, **28**(1), pp 1–9.

Etzioni, A., 1995. *The spirit of community*, London: Fontana.

Evans, G.W., Kantrowitz, G. and Eshelman, P., 2002. 'Housing quality and psychological well-being among the elderly population', *The Journals of Gerontology. Series B, Psychological Sciences and Social Sciences*, **57**(4), pp 381–3.

Evans, S. and Means, R., 2007. *Balanced retirement communities? A case study of Westbury Fields*, Bristol: St Monica Trust.

Evans, S. and Vallelly, S., 2007. *Social well-being in extra care housing*, York: Joseph Rowntree Foundation.

Evans, S., Vallelly, S. and Croucher, K., 2008. 'The role of specialist housing in supporting people with dementia', in M. Downs and B. Bowers (eds), *Excellence in dementia care: research into practice*, Maidenhead: Open University Press/McGraw Hill, pp 319–35.

Everard, K.M., 1999. 'The relationship between reasons for activity and older adult well-being', *Journal of Applied Gerontology*, **18**(3), pp 325–40.

Festinger, L., 1954. 'A theory of social comparison processes', *Human Relations*, **7**(2), pp 117–40.

Fiori, K.L., Antonucci, T.C. and Akiyama, H., 2008. 'Profiles of social relations among older adults: a cross-cultural approach', *Ageing and Society*, **28**(2), pp 203–31.

Flacker, J.M. and Kiely, D.K., 2003. 'Mortality-related factors and 1-year survival in nursing home residents', *Journal of the American Geriatrics Society*, **51**(2), pp 213–21.

Forrest, R. and Bridge, G., 2006. 'What is neighbourliness?', in T. Pilch (ed), *Neighbourliness*, London: The Smith Institute, pp 14–23.

Forrest, R. and Kearns, A., 2001. 'Social cohesion, social capital and the neighbourhood', *Urban Studies*, **38**(12), pp 2125–43.

Fox, M.T. and Gooding, B.A., 1998. 'Physical mobility and social integration: their relationship to the well-being of older Canadians', *Canadian Journal on Aging*, **17**(4), pp 372–83.

Frankenberg, R., 1967. *Communities in Britain: social life in town and country*, London: Penguin Books.

Frankenberg, R., 1982. *Customs and conflict in British society*, Manchester: Manchester University Press.

Gauvin, L. and Spence, J.C., 1996. 'Physical activity and psychological well-being: knowledge base, current issues, and caveats', *Nutrition Review*, **54**(4), part 2, section 53–65.

Gilbart, E.E. and Hirdes, J.P., 2000. 'Stress, social engagement and psychological well-being in institutional settings: evidence based on the Minimum Data Set 2.0', *Canadian Journal on Aging*, **19**(Suppl 2), pp 50–66.

Gilleard, C. and Higgs, P., 2000. *Cultures of ageing: self, citizen and the body*, Harlow: Prentice Hall.

Gilleard, C., Hyde, M. and Higgs, P., 2007. 'The impact of age, place, aging in place and attachment to place on the well-being of the over 50s in England', *Research on Aging*, **29**(6), pp 590–605.

Giuliani, M.V. and Feldman, R., 1993. 'Place attachment in a developmental and cultural context', *Journal of Environmental Psychology*, **13**, pp 267–74.

Godfrey, M., Townsend, J. and Denby, T., 2004. *Building a good life for older people in local communities: the experience of ageing in time and place*, York: Joseph Rowntree Foundation.

Gosschalk, B. and Hatter, W., 1996. 'No sense of place? Changing patterns of local identity', *Demos Quarterly*, **9**, pp 13–16.

Grant, B., 2006. 'Retirement villages: an alternative form of housing on an ageing landscape', *Social Policy Journal of New Zealand*, **27**, pp 100–13.

Gurney, C., and Means, R., 1993. 'The meaning of home in later life', in S. Arber and M. Evandrou (eds), *Ageing, independence, and the life course*, London: Jessica Kingsley Publishers, pp 119–31.

Haas III, W.H. and Serow, W.J., 2002. 'The baby boom, amenity retirement migration, and retirement communities: will the golden age of retirement continue?', *Research on Aging*, **24**(1), pp 150–64.

Harasim, L.M., 1993. *Networlds: networks as social space*, Cambridge, MA: MIT Press.

Hart, J., 2008. *Driven to excess: impacts of motor vehicle traffic on residential quality of life in Bristol, UK*, Bristol: University of the West of England.

Hay, R., 1998. 'Sense of place in developmental context', *Journal of Environmental Psychology*, **18**(1), pp 5–29.

Heller, T., Miller, A.B. and Factor, A., 1998. 'Environmental characteristics of nursing homes and community-based settings, and the well-being of adults with intellectual disability', *Journal of Intellectual Disability Research*, **42**(5), pp 418–28.

Helpguide, 2008. 'Payment options for senior housing and residential care', Helpguide, at www.helpguide.org/elder/paying_for_senior_housing_residential_care.htm

Help the Aged, 2008a. 'Older people in the UK', Help the Aged, at www.helptheaged.org.uk/NR/rdonlyres/318C26CA-F4EB-4A91-B77C-A2867F85AF63/0/uk_facts.pdf

Help the Aged, 2008b. *On my doorstep: communities and older people*, London: Help the Aged.

Help the Aged, 2008c. *Towards common ground: a manifesto for lifetime neighbourhoods*, London: Help the Aged.

Henderson, P., 2003. 'The place of neighbourhood in regeneration and social inclusion policies', *Journal of Community Work and Development*, **1**(4), pp 30–44.

Heywood, F., Oldman, C. and Means, R., 2001. *Housing and home in later life*. Buckingham: Open University Press.

Hickman, M., Crowley, H. and Mai, N., 2008. *Immigration and social cohesion in the UK. The rhythms and realities of everyday life*, York: Joseph Rowntree Foundation.

Hill, A., 2008. 'How our villages are fighting to stay alive', *The Observer*, News, 14 September.

Hillman, S., 2002. 'Participatory singing for older people: a perception of benefit', *Health Education*, **102**(4), pp 163–71.

Ho, H.K., Matsubayashi, K., Wada, T., Kimura, M., Yano, S., Otsuka, K., Fujisawa, M., Kita, T. and Saijoh, K., 2003. 'What determines the life satisfaction of the elderly? Comparative study of residential care home and community in Japan', *Geriatrics and Gerontology International*, **3**(2), pp 79–85.

Hoggett, P., 1997. *Contested communities: experiences, struggles, policies*, Bristol: The Policy Press.

Holmes, C., 2006. *Mixed communities: success and sustainability*, York: Joseph Rowntree Foundation.

Hopkins, L., Thomas, J., Meredyth, D. and Ewing, S., 2004. 'Social capital and community building through an electronic network', *Australian Journal of Social Issues*, **39**(4), pp 369–80.

House, J.S., Kahn, R.L., McLeod, J.D. and Williams, D., 1985. 'Measures and concepts of social support', in S. Cohen and S.L. Syme (eds), *Social support and health*, New York: Academic Press, pp 83–108.

Housing 21, 2007. *Internal report: Care and wellbeing 2007*, London: Housing 21.

Housing Corporation, 2008. *Investing for lifetimes: strategy for housing in an ageing society*, London: The Stationery Office.

Hwang, F., Williams, N. and Batson, H., 2008. 'Improving computer interaction for older users: investigating dynamic on screen targets', SPARC, at www.sparc.ac.uk/media/downloads/executivesummaries/exec_summary_hwang.pdf

icWales, 2007. 'Retirement flats will be "like a holiday"', at www.walesonline.co.uk/map_icwales_art_2007-08-01_5.xml

Imrie, R. and Raco, M., 2003. *Urban renaissance?: New Labour, community and urban policy*, Bristol: The Policy Press.

Jagger, C., Spiers, N. and Matthews, R. with Robinson, T., Lindesay, J., Brayne, C., Comas-Herrera, A., Croft, P. , 2006. *Compression or expansion of disability? Forecasting future disability levels under changing patterns of disease*, London: Kings Fund.

Johnson, M.J., Jackson, N.C., Arnette, J.K. and Koffman, S.D., 2005. 'Gay and lesbian perceptions of discrimination in retirement care facilities', *Journal of Homosexuality*, **49**(2), pp 83–102.

Jones, A., 2006. *Beyond sheltered accommodation: a review of extra care housing and care home provision for BME elders*, London: Age Concern Reports.

Judge, J.O., Whipple, R.H. and Wolfson, L.I., 1994. 'Effects of resistive and balance exercises on isokinetic strength in older persons', *Journal of the American Geriatrics Society*, **42**(9), pp 937–46.

Kahn, R.L. and Antonucci, T., 1980. 'Convoys over the life course: attachment, roles and social support', in P.B. Baltes and O. Brim (eds), *Life-span development and behavior, Vol 3*, 4th edn, Boston, MA: Lexington Press, pp 253-86.

Kane, R.A., Lum, T.Y., Cutler, L.J., Degenholtz, H.B. and Yu, T.C., 2007. 'Resident outcomes in small-house nursing homes: a longitudinal evaluation of the initial green house program', *Journal of the American Geriatrics Society*, **55**(6), pp 832–9.

Kasarda, J.D. and Janowitz, M., 1974. 'Community attachment in mass society', *American Sociological Review*, **39**(3), pp 328–39.

Katz, J.E., Rice, R.E. and Aspden, P., 2001. 'The internet, 1995–2000: access, civic involvement, and social interaction', *American Behavioral Scientist*, **45**(3), pp 405–19.

Kearns, A. and Forrest, R., 2000. 'Social cohesion and multilevel urban governance', *Urban Studies*, **37**(5), pp 995–1017.

Kearns, A. and Mason, P., 2007. 'Mixed tenure communities and neighbourhood quality', *Housing Studies*, **22**(5), pp 661–91.

King, N., 2004. 'Models of extra care and retirement communities', Factsheet 4, for Housing LIN, London: Care Services Improvement Partnership, at www.dhcarenetworks.org.uk/_library/Resources/Housing/Housing_advice/Models_of_Extra_Care_and_Retirement_Communities_Nigel_King_The_Housing__Support_Partnership_January_2004_updated_August_2004.pdf

King, N. and Mills, J., 2005. *Mixed tenure in extra care housing. A technical brief*, London: Housing LIN, at www.dhcarenetworks.org.uk/IndependentLivingChoices/Housing/Topics/type/resource/?cid=1645

King, N., Garwood, S. and Brown, H., 2005. 'Funding extra care housing', Technical Brief 2, Housing LIN, London: Care Services Improvement Partnership, at www.dhcarenetworks.org.uk/_library/Resources/Housing/Housing_advice/Funding_Extra_Care_Housing_July_2005.pdf

King, R., Warnes, A. and Williams, A., 2000. *Sunset lives: British retirement migration to southern Europe*, Oxford: Berg.

Kinsella, A., 2006. *Switched on to telecare: providing health and care support through home based telecare monitoring in the UK and the US*, London: Housing LIN.

Kleinhans, R., 2004. 'Social implications of housing diversification in urban renewal: a review of recent literature', *Journal of Housing and the Built Environment*, **19**(4), pp 367–90.

Kuhn, M., 1977. *Maggie Kuhn on ageing*, Philadelphia: Westminster.

Lawson, S. and Nutter, D., 2008. 'Technology to support ageing in place', Reading: SPARC, at www.sparc.ac.uk/media/downloads/executivesummaries/exec_summary_lawson.pdf

Lee, D. and Newby, H., 1983. *The problem of sociology*, Hemel Hempstead: George Allen and Unwin.

Lee, M., 2006. *Promoting mental health and wellbeing in later life: a first report from the UK inquiry into mental health and wellbeing*, London: Mental Health Foundation and Age Concern.

Levitas, R., 2000. 'Community, Utopia and New Labour', *Local Economy*, **15**(3), pp 188–97.

Leyden, K.M., 2003. 'Social capital and the built environment: the importance of walkable neighborhoods', *American Journal of Public Health*, **93**(9), pp 1546–51.

Livingston, M., Bailey, N. and Kearns, A., 2008. *People's attachment to place: the influence of neighbourhood deprivation*, York: Joseph Rowntree Foundation.

Livingstone, D.N., 1995. 'The spaces of knowledge: contributions towards a historical geography of science', *Environment and Planning D*, **13**(1), pp 5–34.

Low, S.M. and Altman, I., 1992. *Place attachment*, New York: Plenum Press.

Lucco, A.J., 1987. 'Planned retirement housing preferences of older homosexuals', *Journal of Homosexuality*, **14**(3-4), pp 35–56.

Maciver, R.M. and Page, C.H., 1950, *Society: an introductory analysis*, Oxford: Macmillan.

Marsh, P., 2006. 'The Halifax "neighbours" survey', in T. Pilch (ed), *Neighbourliness*, London: The Smith Institute, pp 38–43.

McCafferty, P., 1994. *Living independently: a study of the housing needs of elderly and disabled people*, London: HMSO.

Means, R., 2007. 'Safe as houses? Ageing in place and vulnerable older people in the UK', *Social Policy and Administration*, **41**(1), pp 65–85.

Means, R., Smith, R. and Richards, S., 2003. *Community care: policy and practice*, London: Macmillan.

Meegan, R. and Mitchell, A., 2001. '"It's not community round here, it's neighbourhood": neighbourhood change and cohesion in urban regeneration policies', *Urban Studies*, **38**(12), pp 2167–94.

Ministry of Social Development, 2001. *Positive ageing in New Zealand: diversity, participation and change*, Wellington, NZ: Ministry of Social Development.

Minton, A., 2006. 'Space invaders', *RICS Business*, at www.rics.org/Knowledgezone/Researchandreports/privatisation_public230306.htm

Montgomery, J., 2006. 'Renewing neighbourhoods: strengthening neighbourliness', in T. Pilch (ed), *Neighbourliness*, London: The Smith Institute, pp 44–53.

Munro, G., 1995. *Sense of place in towns, historic buildings as cultural icons, sharing the earth* (ed Fladmark, J.M.), London: Donhead,.

Nash, V. and Christie, I., 2003. *Making sense of community*, London: Institute for Public Policy Research.

Ng, S.H., Kam, P.K. and Pong, R.W.M., 2005. 'People living in ageing buildings: their quality of life and sense of belonging', *Journal of Environmental Psychology*, **25**(3), pp 347–60.

Nicholson, A., 2008. 'Design principles for extra care housing', Factsheet 6, for Housing LIN, London: Care Services Improvement Partnership, at www.dhcarenetworks.org.uk/IndependentLivingChoices/Housing/Topics/type/resource/?cid=5145

Nolan, N.R., Davies, S., Brown, J., Keady, J. and Nolan, J., 2004. 'Beyond person-centred care: a new vision for gerontological nursing', *Journal of Clinical Nursing*, **13**(3a), pp 45–53.

Ochalla, B., 2007. 'The senior situation: the truth about elder care for the GLBT community', *GayWired*, 11 December.

ODPM (Office of the Deputy Prime Minister), 2003a. *New deal for communities*, London: The Stationery Office.

ODPM, 2003b. *Sustainable communities: building for the future*, London: The Stationery Office.

ODPM, 2006. *The social exclusion of older people: evidence from the first wave of the English Longitudinal Survey of Ageing*, London: ODPM.

Oldenburg, R., 1999. *The great good place: cafes, coffee shops, bookstores, bars, hair salons, and other hangouts at the heart of a community*, New York: Marlowe.

ONS (Office for National Statistics) 2007. *Internet access 2007: households and individuals*, London: HMSO.

Owen, T., 2006. *My home life: quality of life in care homes*, London: Help the Aged.

Page, D. and Boughton, R., 1997. *Mixed tenure housing estates: a study undertaken for Notting Hill*, London: NHHT.

Pahl, R.E., 1970. *Patterns of urban life*, London: Brill.

Papadopoulos, R.K., 1999. 'Storied community as secure base: response to the paper by Nancy Caro Hollander "Exile: paradoxes of loss and creativity"', *British Journal of Psychotherapy*, **15**(3), pp 322–32.

Pastalan, L.A. and Barnes, J.E., 1999. 'Personal rituals: identity, attachment to place and community solidarity, in B. Schwarz and R. Brent (eds), *Aging, autonomy and architecture: advances in assisted living*, Baltimore: Johns Hopkins University Press, pp 81–89.

Patel, N., 1999. 'Black and minority ethnic elderly: perspectives on long term care of the elderly', in Royal Commission on Long-term Care for the Elderly (ed), *With respect to old age, vol 1*, London: HMSO, pp 257–304.

Peace, S.M. and Holland, C., 2001. *Inclusive housing in an ageing society: innovative approaches*, Bristol: The Policy Press.

Percival, J., 2001. 'Self-esteem and social motivation in age-segregated settings', *Housing Studies*, **16**(6), pp 827–40.

Phillipson, C., 1997. 'Social relationships in later life: a review of the research literature', *International Journal of Geriatric Psychiatry*, **12**(5), pp 505–12.

Phillipson, C., 2007. 'The elected and the excluded. Sociological perspectives on the experience of place and community in old age', *Ageing and Society*, **27**(3), pp 321–42.

PMSU (Prime Minister's Strategy Unit), 2008. *Realising Britain's potential: future strategic challenges for Britain*, London: Cabinet Office.

Porter, S. and Seeley, C., 2008. *Promoting intergenerational understanding through community philosophy*, York: Joseph Rowntree Foundation.

Potts, M.K., 1997. 'Social support and depression among older adults living alone: the importance of friends within and outside of a retirement community', *Social Work*, **42**(4), pp 348–62.

Prince, M., Harwood, R., Thomas, A. and Mann, A., 1998. 'A prospective population based cohort study of the effects of disablement and social milieu on the onset and maintenance of late life depression', *Psychological Medicine*, **28**(2), pp 337–50.

Putnam, R.D., 1995. 'Tuning in, tuning out: the strange disappearance of social capital in America', *Political Science and Politics*, **28**(4), pp 664–83.

Putnam, R.D., 2000. *Bowling alone: the collapse and revival of American community*, New York: Simon & Schuster.

Raco, M., 2003. 'New Labour, community and the future of Britain's urban renaissance', in R. Imrie and M. Raco (eds), *Urban renaissance? New Labour, community and urban policy*, Bristol: The Policy Press, pp 235–50.

Regnier, V., 2002. *Design for assisted living: guidelines for housing the physically and mentally frail*, New York: Wiley.

Rheingold, H., 1993. 'A slice of life in my virtual community: Global networks: computers and international communication', in P. Ludlow (ed), *High noon on the electric frontier: conceptual issues in cyberspace*, Cambridge: MIT Press, pp 413–36.

Ridings, C.M., Gefen, D. and Arinze, B., 2002. 'Some antecedents and effects of trust in virtual communities', *Journal of Strategic Information Systems*, **11**(3–4), pp 271–95.

Riseborough, M. and Fletcher, P., 2004. *Extra care housing: what is it?* Factsheet 1; DH/CSIP, London: Housing LIN, at www.dhcarenetworks.org.uk/IndependentLivingChoices/Housing/Topics/type/resource/?cid=1633

Robertson, D., Smyth, J. and McIntosh, I., 2008. *Neighbourhood identity: people, time and place*, York: Joseph Rowntree Foundation.

Rogers, R.G., 1999. *Towards a strong urban renaissance*, London: Spon Press.

Rowlands, R., Murie, A. and Tice, A., 2006. *More than tenure mix: developer and purchaser attitudes to new housing estates*, York: Chartered Institute of Housing/Joseph Rowntree Foundation.

Rowles, G.D., 1983. 'Place and personal identity in old age: observations from Appalachia', *Journal of Environmental Psychology*, **3**(4), pp 299–313.

Rubinstein, R.L. and Parmelee, P.A., 1992. 'Attachment to place and the representation of the life course by the elderly', in I. Altman and S.M. Low (eds), *Place attachment: human behavior and environment*, New York, NY: Plenum Press, pp 139–64.

Sampson, R.J., 1988. 'Local friendship ties and community attachment in mass society: a multilevel systemic model', *American Sociological Review*, **53**(5), pp 766–79.

Sanchez, M., 2008. *Intergenerational programmes: towards a society for all ages*, Barcelona: La Caixa Foundation.

Sandwell Metropolitan Borough Council, 2008. *Extra care housing: a modern approach*, at www.laws.sandwell.gov.uk/ccm/navigation/health-and-social-care/social-services/housing-and-your-home/extra-care-housing/extra-care-housing--a-modern-approach/

Sangster, K., 1997. *Costing lifetime homes*, York: Joseph Rowntree Foundation.

Sarkissian, W., Forsyth, A. and Heine, W., 1990. 'Residential "social mix": the debate continues', *Australian Planner*, **28**(1), pp 5–16.

Savage, M., Bagnall, G. and Longhurst, B., 2005. *Globalization and belonging*, New York: Sage Publications.

Scott, J.K. and Johnson, T.G., 2005. 'Bowling alone but online together: social capital in e-communities', *Journal of the Community Development Society*, **36**(1), pp 1–17.

Seabrook, J., 1984. *The idea of neighbourhood: what local politics should be about*, London: Pluto.

Shankle, M.D., Maxwell, C.A., Katzman, E.S. and Landers, S., 2003. 'An invisible population: older lesbian, gay, bisexual, and transgender individuals', *Clinical Research and Regulatory Affairs*, **20**(2), pp 159–82.

Sherman, S.R., 1975. 'Patterns of contacts for residents of age-segregated and age-integrated housing', *Journal of Gerontology*, **30**(1), pp 103–7.

Shirky, C., 1995. *Voices from the net*, Emeryville, CA: Ziff-Davis Press.

Shumaker, S.A. and Taylor, R.B., 1983. 'Toward a clarification of people-place relationships: a model of attachment to place', in N.R. Feimer and E.S. Geller (eds), *Environmental psychology: directions and perspectives*, New York: Praeger, pp 219–51.

Skjaeveland, O. and Garling, T. 1997. 'Effects of interactional space on neighbouring', *Journal of Environmental Psychology*, **17**(3), pp 181–98.

Smee, J., 2008. 'Glad to be gay and gray in Berlin's new old people's homes', *The Guardian*, 17 March.

Social Exclusion Unit, 1998. *Bringing Britain together: a national strategy for neighbourhood renewal*, London: The Stationery Office.

Social Exclusion Unit, 2000. *National strategy for neighbourhood renewal: a framework for consultation*, London: Cabinet Office.

Stacey, M., 1969. 'The myth of community studies', *British Journal of Sociology*, **20**(2), pp 134–47.

Stacey-Konnert, C. and Pynoos, J., 1992. 'Friendship and social networks in a continuing care retirement community', *Journal of Applied Gerontology*, **11**(3), pp 298–313.

Stokowski, P.A., 2002. 'Languages of place and discourses of power: constructing new senses of place', *Journal of Leisure Research*, **34**(4), pp 368–83.

Sugihara, S. and Evans, G.W., 2000. 'Place attachment and social support at continuing care retirement communities', *Environment and Behavior*, **32**(3), pp 400–9.

Sugisawa, H., Shibata, H., Hougham, G.W., Sugihara, Y. and Liang, J., 2002. 'The impact of social ties on depressive symptoms in US and Japanese elderly', *Journal of Social Issues*, **58**(4), pp 785–804.

Sustainable Development Commission, 2006. 'Health, place and nature: how outdoor environments influence health and well-being', London: Sustainable Development Commission, at www.sd-commission.org.uk/publications.php

Sutherland, S., 1999. *With respect to old age: long term care – rights and responsibilities: a report by the Royal Commission on Long Term Care*, London: The Stationery Office.

Sweetinburgh, S. and King, N., 2007. *Catering arrangements in extra care housing*, London: Housing LIN.

Tait, C. and Fuller, E., 2002. *Health survey for England 2000: psychosocial wellbeing among older people*, London: The Stationery Office.

Taylor, M., 2003. 'Community issues and social networks', in C. Phillipson, G. Allan and D.H.J. Morgan (eds), *Social networks and social exclusion*, Aldershot: Ashgate, pp 205–18.

Taylor, M., 2008. *Transforming disadvantaged places: effective strategies for places and people*, York: Joesph Rowntree Foundation.

Thomas, D.N., 1983. *The making of community work*, London: Allen and Unwin.

Tinker, A., Hanson, J., Wright, F., Mayagoitia, R., Wojgani, H. and Holmans, A., 2007. *Remodelling sheltered housing and residential care homes to extra care housing: advice to housing and care providers*, London: Kings College.

Tönnies, F. and Loomis, C.P., 1957. *Community and society (Gemeinschaft und Gesellschaft)*, Michigan: Michigan State University Press.

Turner, B., 2007. 'The enclave society: towards a sociology of immobility', *European Journal of Social Theory*, **10**(2), pp 287–303.

United Seniors Health Council, 2002. *Planning for long term care*, Washington: McGraw Hill.

Uzzell, D., Pol, E. and Badenas, D., 2002. 'Place identification, social cohesion, and environmental sustainability', *Environment and Behavior*, **34**(1), pp 26–52.

Vallelly, S., Evans, S., Fear, T. and Means, R., 2006. *Opening doors to independence: a longitudinal study exploring the contribution of extra care housing to the care and support of older people with dementia*, London: Housing 21.

Ward-Thompson, C. and Sugiyama, T., 2006. *The relationship between older people's quality of life, outdoor activity and outdoor environments*, Presentation, www.idgo. ac.uk/researchpresentations.htm

Warr, P., Butcher, V. and Robertson, I., 2004. 'Activity and psychological well-being in older people', *Ageing and Mental Health*, **8**(2), pp 172–83.

Watts, B., 2008. *What are today's social evils? The results of a web consultation*, York: Joseph Rowntree Foundation.

Webster, C., 2002. 'Property rights and the public realm: gates, green belts and gemeinschaft', *Environment and Planning B*, **29**(3), pp 315–26.

Weiss, R.S., 1974. 'The provisions of social relations', in Z. Rubin (ed), *Doing unto others*, Englewood Cliffs: Prentice Hall, pp 17–26.

Wellman, B. and Gulia, M., 1999. 'Net surfers don't ride alone: virtual communities as communities', in M. Smith and P. Kollock (eds), *Communities in cyberspace*, London: Routledge, pp 167–94.

Wenger, C.G., 1995. 'A comparison of urban with rural support networks: Liverpool and North Wales', *Ageing and Society*, **15**(1), pp 59–81.

Willmott, P., 1989. *Community initiatives: patterns and prospects*, London: Policy Studies Institute.

Wilton, R.D., 1998. 'The constitution of difference: space and psyche in landscapes of exclusion', *Geoforum*, **29**(2), pp 173–85.

Woolever, C., 1992. 'A contextual approach to neighbourhood attachment', *Urban Studies*, **29**(1), pp 99–116.

World Health Organization (WHO), 2006. *Global age friendly cities project*, Geneva: WHO.

Worley, C., 2005. '"It's not about race. It's about the community": New Labour and "community cohesion"', *Critical Social Policy*, **25**(4), pp 483–96.

Index

A

Abrams, P. 14, 94
activities *see* social activities
actuarial fees model 48-9
adult education 65, 110
'affinity communities' in US 64-5
affordable housing
  as new build requirement 18, 55
  shared ownership options 46, 50, 54, 101
age
  and experience of community 21-9
  mix of ages in retirement villages 49
  see also age segregation; ageism
Age Concern 53, 99
age segregation 131-2, 133-4
  age-restricted residency 2, 105-6, 121-2
  and ageism 108
  and community 5, 6, 105-6, 131
  and diversity 105-6, 107, 121-2, 130, 131
  and financial viability 122
Age-Friendly Cities initiative (WHO) 24, 83,
    112, 126
ageing population statistics 2, 31, 127, 128
  see also demographics of ageing society
ageism 108, 127
Aldridge, F. 110
Allan, G. 13
Altman, I. 107-8
Anderson, B. 27
anti-social behaviour and tenure mix 18, 100,
    107
Antonucci, T.C. 8, 9
'Apartment for Life' in Denmark 68
Ashida, S. 131
Askham, J. 28
assistive technologies 89, 114, 123, 136
Atchley, R.C. 83
Atkinson, R. 16, 17
Audit Commission 132
Australia 66, 68, 104
Avenidas Village, California 64

B

'baby boomers' as retirees 60, 109, 118, 128
Barton Mews, Staffordshire 118-20
Beacon Hill village, Boston 63
Beech, R. 114
belonging and community 9, 10, 126-7
  age and attachment to place 23, 26
  importance for older people 21-2, 23, 26
  and length of residence 12, 21, 26, 126
  as motive for moving 3, 25, 26-7, 28, 129
Berkman, L.F. 75
Bernard, M. 25, 71-2, 81, 103, 108, 131
Berryhill village, Staffordshire 96
Biggs, S. 26, 27, 52, 73
black and minority ethnic groups 98-9, 107
Blacksburg Electronic Village 116
Blakely, E.J. 52
Blanchard, A. 116

Blandy, S. 52, 73, 87, 89, 132
Blechman, A. 62-3, 132
Boughton, R. 18, 101
Bourdieu, P. 16
Bournville estate 100
Brent, J. 10, 16, 129
Bridge, G. 13-14
Buckshaw retirement village, Lancs 98
built environment *see* design and built
    environment
Bulmer, M. 14, 94
Burholt, V. 117
Burnett, J. 15

C

Cadbury, G. 100
Cahill, S. 103, 104
Calhoun, C.J. 10, 11
Callendar Court, Gateshead 44-5
Campbell, D.T. 94, 102, 131
care homes *see* residential care
care provision
  care packages 35, 62
  dementia units 78
  and fee structures 48-9, 62
  flexible care options 3, 49, 51, 84
  in US 62
  funding sources 41, 78
  levels of care and housing type 2, 34*tab*, 49-50,
    95-7, 106-7, 118-20
  person-centred care 136, 139, 140
  providers 38-9, 41, 43
  telecare planning 89
  see also staffing and care provision
casual social interaction 76, 79, 87, 102
CCRCs *see* continuing care retirement
    communities
change
  and attitudes towards home 28
  see also social change
Cheshire, P. 54
Chinese community 99
choice
  and financial status 52, 100, 132, 133
  and place attachment 90
civic engagement opportunities 84
Clough, R. 27, 105
cognitive function impairment 5, 76, 77, 88-9
Cohen, A.P. 9
co-housing in Europe 67, 118, 129
Colclough, G. 11-12
Colker, D. 104
Colliers Court, Bristol 99
Commission for Social Care Inspection (CSCI)
    38
communal facilities and social interaction 81-2,
    88, 102
communities of interest 9, 10, 11, 18, 19, 26, 28,
    52, 131
  'affinity communities' in US 64-5

and marketing for retirement villages 3, 33, 93, 130, 133
neglect by public policy 16
'communities of the mind' 9, 26
community
  complexity of 12, 17, 126
  concepts of and theories on 4, 7-19, 72, 125-6
    and diversity 94, 131
    personal perceptions 52, 73
  definitions 8, 10, 72, 125
  dual meaning and difficulties of defining 11
  and housing 17-18
  housing with care settings as communities 1, 5, 71-91, 131
  loss of community theme 7-8, 24-5
  negative aspects 16, 19, 72, 131
  nostalgia for past communities 11, 17, 25, 26, 125
  and public policy 7, 13-16, 72, 83
  see also local community; sense of community
community cohesion 13, 14, 15, 72, 83
  see also social cohesion
Community Cohesion Unit 15
community engagement 109-10, 112, 113, 122-3
'community in place' theory 19, 126, 129
community of place theories 8-9
  see also place attachment and community
complex communities concept 12, 17, 126
computer access 115-17, 123, 127
  see also internet
continuing care retirement communities (CCRCs) 48-9, 51, 62, 95, 106
control factor 26, 27, 126-7, 129
core and cluster retirement village model 48
costs of development
  extra care housing 40-1
  funding sources 40-1, 42-3, 50, 56-7, 118
  retirement villages 50-1, 54, 65
crime *see* fear of crime; security
Croucher, K. 25, 49, 52, 73, 76, 98, 104
Crow, G. 13

D

Darton, R. 99
Daum, M. 105
Davies, W.K.D. 14
dementia and housing with care settings 3, 47, 97-8, 106
  integrated models 77, 97
  segregated models 33, 77-8, 97
  and social interaction 11, 74, 88-9
  design factors 77-8, 135-6
  specialist schemes/units 33, 78, 97, 98
demographics of ageing society 2, 31, 122
  international context 60, 66
  and minority ethnic groups 99
  see also ageing population statistics
Denham Garden village, Bucks 52, 94
Denmark 67-8, 129
Department of Communities and Local Government (DCLG) 13, 104
Department of Health
  funding and grants 40, 96

Housing LIN standards 35-6, 51, 79
  telecare planning 89
Department for Work and Pensions (DWP):
  Opportunity age 140
depression 10-11, 74, 79
deprived communities 13, 16, 83
design and built environment
  and concept of home 27, 126
  and extra care housing 46, 77-8, 79, 120, 139
  and healthy ageing 83, 84, 112
  and independent living 37, 47, 111, 135
  mixed tenure and 'tenure blind' approach 6, 103
  and public policy 17-18, 19
  and quality of life 3, 4-5, 22, 24, 112
  segregation of mixed tenures 102-3
  and sense of community 76-90, 102-3
  and social interaction 76-9, 102, 107, 126, 135-6
  see also new housing development
Despres, C. 27
Devon Senior Council 122-3
discrimination 103-4, 108, 127
dispersed facilities retirement village model 48
diversity
  and community 16, 131
  and healthy ageing 83
  and housing with care settings 5-6, 93-108, 136-8, 140
  and ethnic background 98-9, 107
  and gender and sexuality 103-4
  and health status 95-8
  and segregation by age 93, 105-6, 107, 121-2, 130, 131-2
  and socio-economic background 96, 100-3, 107
  see also mixed communities; mixed tenure
domiciliary care 38
Durkheim, E. 8, 74

E

Eales, J. 84
Edwards, C. 16
Elderly Accommodation Counsel (EAC) 25, 32, 37
'elective belonging' 22, 129
environment
  environmentally friendly retirement villages in US 65, 67, 120-1
  social change and older people 111
  see also local communities
environmental psychology theories 12-13
  see also place attachment theory
Eshelman, P.E. 27
ethnic background and diversity 98-9, 107
Etzioni, A. 15
Europe 59, 67-8, 129
Evans, G.W. 17, 26, 27
Evans, S.
  balanced retirement communities study (with Means) 3-4, 18, 25, 53, 73-4, 75, 80, 81-2, 87, 88-9, 95-6, 101-2, 103, 105-6, 108, 136-8
  housing for people with dementia 97, 135-6

social wellbeing and extra care housing study (with Vallelly) 3, 4, 74, 75, 76, 77, 81, 82, 84, 87-8, 96, 98, 103, 138-40
Everard, K.M. 82
exercise and design of built environment 78-9
Extra Care Charitable Trust 39, 54
extra care housing 1, 35-47, 56
  age-restricted residency 105
  care provision 38-9, 89
    levels of 2, 96-7, 106-7
  costs 40-1
  definition and defining features 33, 34*tab*, 35-7
  design and built environment 46, 77-8, 79, 120, 139
  differences from retirement villages 2-3, 35, 132-3
  and diversity 93, 99, 130, 140
  family carers and provision for 88, 138
  and financial status 28
  health status and dependency levels 96-7
  history and development 32-3, 35
  and interaction with local community 2-3, 84, 121, 139
  popularity 46-7
  promotion of sense of community 71, 72, 87
  public funding 42-3, 56, 78, 117
  recent developments 41-6, 118-20
  remodelling existing stock as 44-5
  residents with dementia 3, 97-8, 135-6
  and security 87
  services and facilities 44, 45, 46, 81, 117, 139
    community health services in 118-20
  sites for development 2-3, 44, 45, 118
  size of developments 2, 34*tab*, 128
    larger developments/villages 28, 35, 37, 39-40, 121
  and social change 6, 117-22, 123-4, 133
  and social interaction and wellbeing 4, 75, 138-40
  tenure types 34*tab*, 39-40, 43, 101
  variety of terms for 34*tab*, 35
  see also staffing and care provision
Extra Care Housing Fund 42-3

F

facilities *see* services and facilities
family
  and benefits of social interaction 75, 88, 138
  as carers and quality of life 4, 88
  and intergenerational contact 105, 107
  maintaining relationships with 84
  proximity and sense of community 12, 16
  and support network 9
Fear, T. 3, 135-6
fear of crime 27, 52, 53, 106
  and fear of young people 25, 106, 128
fee structures 48-9, 62
Feldman, R. 12, 23, 89
finance models 48-9, 62, 65, 66, 90
  public–private finance 118-19, 120
financial status and housing options 28, 46, 48-9, 62
  lack of choice for less well-off 52, 100, 132

retirement villages as option for 'well-off' 52, 132
  see also luxury market
Finland 68
Fiori, K.L. 8-9
flexible care options 3, 49, 51, 62, 84
flood-risk areas and older people 111
Fold Housing Association, Northern Ireland 89
Forrest, R. 13-14, 15, 131, 132
4Children 130
Fox, M.T. 75
Frankenberg, R. 10
friends 12, 73, 74, 75, 83, 84, 138
  see also social interaction; social networks theory
fully serviced apartment model 49-50, 57, 95
further education 65, 110
'future proofing' of new housing 32, 47, 83, 112, 117

G

gardens and social interaction 79-80
gated communities 5, 52-4, 87, 89, 132
Gateshead Council 36, 42, 44-5
Gauvin, L. 78
gay and lesbian residents and communities 64, 66, 103-4, 107, 118
gemeinschaft and *gesellschaft* 8, 125
gender differences 75-6, 82, 104
Gilleard, C. 10, 11, 19, 22
Giuliani, M.V. 12, 23, 89
globalisation and community 10, 22
Godfrey, M. 75
Gooding, B.A. 75
Gosschalk, B. 108
government *see* public policy and community
'green house' concept and dementia 98, 106
Green Park village, Reading 56
green retirement villages in US 65, 67, 120-1
Gulia, M. 116
Gurney, C. 27-8
Gyngemosegard community, Denmark 67-8

H

Haas III, W.H. 118
Hancock, R. 28
'hard-to-let' housing 31, 41-2, 44-5
Hartfields village, Hartlepool 37
Hartrigg Oaks, York 48-9, 101
Hatter, W. 108
Hay, R. 23
health services in extra care housing scheme 118-20
Health Survey for England 75-6, 82
health and wellbeing
  design of built environment and physical activity 78-9
  frail health and exclusion 73, 75, 77, 80, 127, 140
    benefits of social activities 82-3, 138
    and social wellbeing 138-40
  health status of residents 95-8
  healthy ageing factors 83-4, 112-13

and physical environment 80-1
and social support and interaction 10-11, 21-2, 74-5, 127
see also quality of life; social wellbeing
Heaney, C.A. 131
Help the Aged 88, 111, 112, 113, 123, 127
Herbert, D. 14
Hickman, M. 16, 94
Higgs, P. 10, 11, 22
Highland Green village, Maine 120
Hillman, S. 83
Ho, H.K. 75
Hoggett, P. 17
Holmes, C. 100-1
home 22, 27-8, 37, 126-7, 129
Home Office
  citizenship survey 9
  Community Cohesion Unit 15
home ownership 28, 37, 100
  shared ownership option 46, 50, 54, 101
HomeBuy scheme 101
Homes and Communities Agency 128
Horan, T. 116
'hotel-style' model 49-50, 57, 62, 95
House, J.S. 11
housing
  and concept of community 17-18
  and demands of ageing population 31-2, 128
  poor condition 22, 41-2, 126
  see also design and built environment; new housing development
housing associations 40, 50, 101
Housing Corporation 40, 42
Housing Learning and Improvement Network (LIN) 35-6, 51, 79, 86, 120
housing market and retirement properties 65, 122
Housing Strategy for an Ageing Society 23-4, 32, 83, 94, 100, 111, 122
Housing 21 36, 44, 46, 78, 86, 96-7, 103
housing with care settings 1, 31-57
  and ageing and experience of community 26-8, 73-4
  change and future of 117-22, 131-2, 133
  definitions and models of 33, 34*tab*
  demand for 123-4
  distinguishing features 2-3, 35
  and diversity 93-108, 121-2, 130, 131, 136-8, 140
  history and development 5, 32-3
  international context 5, 52-3
  and older people's need for community 26-8
  and sense of community 71-91, 126
  see also extra care housing; retirement villages
How is Your Home? questionnaire 25

I
identity and community 9, 10, 11, 18, 19
  age and attachment to place 23, 26
  and concept of home 22, 27-8, 126
  and desire of older people for community 27, 129
  and online communities 115

and social interaction 75
  see also place attachment and community
'imagined communities' 27
Imrie, R. 15
independence and policy 37, 111, 127, 135-6
independent living model 49, 95, 137
India: retirement villages 67
indoor spaces and sense of community 76-7
information and advice 37, 113
Institute of Public Policy Research 9
interest-based communities *see* communities of interest
intergenerational contact 105-6, 107, 130-1, 131-2, 133-4
intergenerational housing schemes in Europe 67-8, 129, 132, 134
internet 6, 109, 112, 114-17, 127-8
  access and social interaction 82, 123
  online communities 10, 12, 114-17
isolation and loneliness 24, 25, 73, 74, 87
  and gender 75-6, 82, 103

J
Janowitz, M. 12
Johnson, M.J. 104
Jones, A. 99
Joseph Rowntree Foundation 37, 48-9

K
Kahn, R.L. 9
Kasarda, J.D. 12
Kearns, A. 15, 17, 18, 100, 131, 132
key-worker staffing system 78, 87-8, 140
King, N. 22, 36-7, 40-1, 101
Kinsella, A. 89
Kintrea, K. 17
Kleinhans, R. 18, 100
Kuhn, M. 107, 132

L
Ladyman, S. 53
Laguna Woods Village, California 60
Lee, D. 10
length of residence 12, 21, 26, 126
Levitas, R. 15-16
Leyden, K.M. 79
lifecourse and community 21-9, 72
lifestyle gated communities 52
Lifetime Homes Standard 24, 32, 83, 113
lifetime neighbourhoods 24, 83, 112, 113, 126
Lishman, G. 53
Livingston, M. 89
Livingstone, D.N. 12
local area agreements (LEAs) 15, 112
local authorities 14-15, 50, 122-3
  see also social services
local community
  interaction with wider community
    accessibility factors 86
    extra care housing 2-3, 84, 121, 139
    gated communities 87, 132
    health services in extra care housing scheme 118-20

impact of retirement villages 62-3, 84-6, 122, 129
and quality of life 3, 83
retirement villages 62-3, 76, 84, 121, 122, 127-8, 129
and sense of community 76, 83-90
and social wellbeing 4, 5, 9, 76, 83, 139
naturally occurring retirement communities 63-4, 121, 133
social change and older people 6, 29, 109-12, 113, 133
closure of services 110, 111, 117, 122, 127
see also neighbourhood
location *see* sites for development
loneliness *see* isolation and loneliness
Loomis, C.P. 8, 74
Lovat Fields, Milton Keynes 39-40, 54
Low, S.M. 107-8
Lucco, A.J. 103-4
luxury market 54, 56-7, 62, 66

M

Maciver, R.M. 10
marketing campaigns
communities of interest/like-mindedness 3, 33, 130, 133
limitations on diversity 93, 94
promoting sense of community 3, 5, 26-7, 71-2, 90, 126, 133
Marsh, P. 9, 73
Mason, P. 17, 18, 100
Means, R. 27-8
balanced retirement communities study (with S. Evans) 3-4, 18, 25, 53, 73-4, 75, 80, 81-2, 87, 88-9, 95-6, 101-2, 103, 105-6, 108, 136-8
extra care housing and dementia study 135-6
Meegan, R. 13
members and non-members 16, 27, 28, 131
men and social interaction 75-6, 82, 103
mental health *see* dementia; depression
Mere View, Suffolk 46
Metsatahti scheme, Finland 68
Mexico 67
Mills, J. 101
Milton Keynes Council Plan 54
minority ethnic groups 98-9, 107
Mitchell, A. 13
mixed communities
age range in retirement villages 49
diversity and policy 94, 100, 107, 130
limitations of 100
policy and built environment 17-18
see also diversity; mixed tenure
mixed tenure 5-6, 130
extra care villages 39-40
and funding arrangements 51
management challenges 50-1, 107
'pepperpotting' approach 6, 40, 103
public policy and community 17-18, 53-4
and diversity 94, 100-3, 107, 130
retirement villages 50-1, 53-4, 57, 101-2
segregation of tenure types 101-2, 102-3
mobility impairment 5, 76, 77, 80, 102, 140

Monica Wills scheme, Bristol 80
mortality rates and social interaction 11, 74
multigenerational communities in Europe 67-8, 129, 132
multiple community membership 11, 22, 126
Munro, G. 9

N

National Dementia Strategy 97
National Framework for Older People 37
National Gay and Lesbian Task Force (US) 64
National Institute of Continuing Education 110
National Strategy for Housing in an Ageing Society 23-4, 32, 83, 94, 100, 111, 122
National Strategy for Neighbourhood Renewal 13, 18
naturally occurring retirement communities (NORCs) in US 63-4, 121, 133
neighbourhood
and community over lifecourse 23, 24
definition and relation to community 13-14, 19
interaction with wider community 83-90
lifetime neighbourhoods initiative 24, 83, 112, 113, 126
naturally occurring retirement communities 63-4, 121, 133
and public policy 13-14, 18, 83
in US 63
and social interaction 14, 72, 73, 131
and physical layout 80
see also local community; neighbours
Neighbourhood Renewal Strategy 13, 18
neighbours 9, 23, 73, 131
Netherlands 67, 68, 129, 132
network mapping and community 8-9
new housing development
affordability of extra care housing 46
affordable housing requirement 18, 55
and ageing population 128-9
and Lifetime Homes Standard 24, 32, 113
mixed tenure 18
retirement villages 54, 118
see also costs of development; design and built environment; sites for development
New Labour: policy and community 13-16, 19, 83, 94
New Zealand 66, 68
Newby, H. 10
Ng, S.H. 23
Nolan, N.R. 88
nominal communities 14
non-members and exclusion 16, 27, 28, 131
nostalgia for past communities 11, 17, 25, 26, 125
not-for-profit providers 50, 59, 101
nursing care home model 49-50, 95

O

Oak Hammond village, Florida 65
Oak House scheme, Ipswich 77, 78
Ochalla, B. 104
Office for National Statistics 123
Oldenburg, R. 82
online communities 10, 12, 114-17

Opportunity Age strategy 21
outdoor spaces 79-81, 113
Owen, T. 75, 88

P

Page, C.H. 10
Page, D. 18, 101
Pahl, R.E. 9, 11, 26
Painswick village, Gloucestershire 84-6
Papadopoulos, R.K. 27
Parmelee, P.A. 22
Patel, N. 99
pavements 112, 113
'pepperpotting' of tenures 6, 40, 103
perception and community 26-7, 52, 73, 102
Percival, J. 105
person-centred care 136, 139, 140
Phillipson, C. 26, 52, 100
physical activity 78-9
physical features and place 9-10
place attachment and community 12-13, 22, 126
    importance for older people 23, 26, 89
    negative aspects 16
    and physical features 9-10
    relevance of 18-19, 72, 126
    remaking of place 129-30
    and sense of community 89-90
    see also identity and community
planning issues 18, 54-5
policy *see* public policy and community
poor housing condition 22, 41-2, 126
Porter, S. 106
prestige gated communities 52
Prime Minister's Strategy Unit (PMSU) 105
Priory Court, Gateshead 35, 36
privacy 73, 86
private developers 40
    and extra care housing 43, 101
    public–private finance 118-19, 120
    and retirement villages 54, 55, 56-7, 122
    in US 59, 65
    and tenure models 50, 101
private finance initiative (PFI) model 50
providers and housing with care settings 34*tab*,
    38-9, 42, 43
    and tenure models 50
public policy
    and community 7, 13-16, 72, 83
    and demands of ageing population 127
    and funding for extra care housing 42-3, 56,
        78, 117-18
    and independence 37, 111, 127, 135-6
    and mixed tenure/communities 17-18, 53-4,
        94, 100-3, 107, 130
    and retirement villages 53-4
    and social wellbeing 140
    see also sustainable communities agenda
public spaces 113
public toilets 112, 113
public transport 84, 110, 112, 113
public–private finance for extra care housing
    scheme 118-19, 120
Putnam, R.D. 11, 16, 22, 74

Q

quality of life
    and design and built environment 3, 4-5, 22,
        24, 112, 126
        for residents with dementia 98, 135-6
    and experience of retirement villages 52
    lessening satisfaction with 21, 127
    see also financial status; health and wellbeing;
        social wellbeing

R

Raco, M. 15, 16
Rainbow Vision community, California 64
registered social landlords 40, 101
remaking of place 129-30
remodelling hard-to-let housing 44-5
research studies 3-4, 135-40
residential care 31-2, 34*tab*, 47, 75-6, 88
    extra care housing as alternative 43-4, 46
retirement villages 1, 47-57
    and belonging to community 3, 25, 26-7, 28,
        129
    and care provision
        and fee structures 48-9, 62
        levels of provision 2, 49-50, 84, 95
    costs of development 50-1, 54, 65
    criticisms 52, 57
    definition and defining features 33, 34*tab*,
        47-50
    dementia and specialist services 98
    differences from extra care housing 2-3, 35,
        132-3
    and diversity 93, 101-2, 108, 130, 136-8
    experience of living in 52-6, 73-4, 102
    and financial status 28, 48-9, 52, 132
    health status and dependency levels 95-6, 121
    history and development 32, 51-2, 54, 118
    international perspective 52-3, 59-69
    leisure and amenity-based developments in US
        60, 61, 68, 93, 107, 118, 130
    and local community 121, 122, 129
        interaction with and sense of community 76,
            84, 127-8
        and services in US 62-3
    luxury market 54, 56-7, 62, 66
    models of 48, 49-50, 95
        in US 61, 120-1
    motives for moving into 3, 25, 26-8, 117, 128,
        129
    out of town sites and community 2-3, 55, 84-6,
        118, 121
    planning and classification 54-5
    popularity 51-2, 54
    and promotion of sense of community 71-2,
        73-4, 84-6, 87, 90
    and public policy 53-4
    services and facilities 28, 32, 34*tab*, 81-2, 85,
        117, 128
        in US 61-2
    size of developments 2, 34*tab*, 35, 47-8, 51, 54,
        127-8
        in US 59, 60
    social activities 85, 138

and social change 6, 117-22, 123-4, 133
social interaction and community 3-4, 73-4, 75
sustainability in long term 132
tenure options 32, 34*tab*, 47
  mixed tenure 50-1, 53-4, 57, 101-2
use of term 'village' 71-2
see also gated communities
Rheingold, H. 115
Richmond village, Coventy 71
Ridings, C.M. 114
risk management 3, 88-9
Roberts, D. 114
Robertson, D. 10, 17, 18, 23, 75
Romans and retirement villages 32, 59
Ros Anders Gard village, Sweden 67
Roseland Parc, Truro 47-8, 71, 93
Rowles, G.D. 22, 23, 129
Royal Commission on Long-Term Care 43
Royal Institute of Chartered Surveyors (RICS)
  53
Rubinstein, R.L. 22
rural settings 55, 84-6, 128
see also villages

S

St Monica Trust *see* Westbury Fields
Sampson, R.J. 13
Sandwell Metropolitan Borough Council 72
Santa Marta village, Kansas 62
Savage, M. 22
Scandinavia 67-8, 129
Seabrook, J. 14
security 52, 86, 87, 89
  see also fear of crime
Seeley, C. 106
segregation
  of gated communities 53, 132
  of tenure types 101-2, 102-3
  see also age segregation
Senior Friendly Neighborhoods (US) 63
sense of community 71-91, 125-8, 133
  and built environment 76-90, 102-3
  definitions 72-3
  and diversity 105-6, 108
  marketing and promotion of 3, 5, 26-7, 71-2,
    87, 90, 126, 133
  as motivating factor 3, 25, 26-7, 28, 129
  and proximity to family 12, 16
  and public policy 83
  and quality of life 5
  residents' views and experiences 73-4, 102
  and social interaction 72, 74-6, 82-3, 85, 87-80,
    90, 130, 131
Serow, W.J. 118
services and facilities 4, 24, 34*tab*, 139
  accessible services and healthy ageing 83, 84,
    112, 113
  accessibility problems 81, 102
  advantages of retirement villages 28, 32
  for development of sense of community 25, 28,
    78, 81-2, 102
  extra care housing 44, 45, 46, 81, 117, 118-20,
    139

and local community
  access to 86, 118
  closure of local services 110, 111, 117, 122,
    127
  for healthy ageing 111-12, 113
  retirement villages 28, 32, 34*tab*, 81-2, 85, 117,
    128
  in US 61-2
  see also care provision
sexual orientation 64, 66, 103-4
Shankle, M.D. 104
shared interests *see* communities of interest
shared ownership options 46, 50, 54, 101
sheltered housing 31, 34*tab*, 41-2
  and extra care housing 43, 44, 56
Sherman, S.R. 105
simple communities concept 12
Sitaraman, B. 11-12
sites for development
  extra care housing 2-3, 44, 45, 118
  retirement villages 2-3, 55-6, 118, 121
size of developments 34*tab*
  extra care housing 2, 28, 35, 37, 39-40, 127
  retirement villages 2, 47-8, 51, 54, 127-8
Smee, J. 104
Snyder, M.G. 52
social activities 78, 80, 82-3, 85, 103, 138
  see also social interaction
social capital 11-12, 13, 16, 72, 74, 125
Social Care Institute for Excellence 114
social change and older people 6, 22, 109-24, 133
  technological change 112, 114-17, 123, 127-8
social cohesion
  and diversity 94, 100, 107
  and gated communities 53, 132
  and mixed tenure 17-18, 53-4, 94, 100, 101,
    107
  and public policy approaches 15, 16, 56, 72
  see also community cohesion
social exclusion
  and community agenda 13, 16
  frail health and exclusion 73, 75, 77, 80, 127,
    140
  non-members and exclusion 16, 27, 28, 131
  older people and local communities 29
social housing *see* registered social landlords;
  social renting
Social Housing Fund 42
social interaction
  and design and built environment 17-18, 19
    accessible design 76-9, 102, 107, 126, 135-6,
      139
    outdoor spaces 79-81
  and gated communities 53, 132
  gender differences 75-6, 82, 103
  as key element of community 10-11
  and mixed tenure/communities 17-18, 51, 94,
    100-1, 102
  as motive for move 26, 27
  and neighbourhood concept 14, 72, 73, 131
  and quality of life and wellbeing 4, 5, 10, 74-6,
    127

and sense of community 72, 74-6, 87-80, 90, 130, 131
  and staffing issues 87-8
  technology and online communities 10, 12, 114-17, 123
  see also friends; social activities; social exclusion
social networking sites 114, 115, 116
social networks theory 8-9, 72, 125, 131
  benefits of social interaction 10-11, 74
  negative aspects of community 16, 131
  number of friends and community 12
  see also social interaction
social renting 18, 34*tab*, 38, 40, 101
social services 38, 39
social support 11, 21-2, 75, 131
social wellbeing 4, 5, 9, 10, 74-6, 88, 127, 138-40
  see also health and wellbeing
socio-economic background 96, 100-3, 107
Sonali Gardens scheme, Tower Hamlets 99
South, K. 103, 104
South Africa 59, 68
Spain 67
Spence, J.C. 78
Stacey, M. 8
staffing and care provision 41, 139
  key-worker system 78, 87-8, 140
  and social interaction opportunities 87-9
  staff training and quality of life 3, 89, 136
Stokowski, P.A. 12
Stratford village, Colorado 62
street layout 17, 80, 86, 113, 139
Strong and Prosperous Communities (White Paper) 7, 15
Sugihara, S. 26
Sugiyama, T. 79
Sun City retirement village, Florida 59
support networks 9
  social support 11, 21-2, 75, 131
Supporting People Administering Authority (SPAA) 41
supportive technologies 114, 115
Sustainable Communities Act (2007) 14-15, 87, 112
sustainable communities agenda 14-15, 17, 56, 83, 111, 132
  and mixed communities 17, 54, 94, 100, 121-2, 130
Sustainable Communities Plan 7, 17, 94
Sustainable Development Commission 80-1
'sustainable urban village' approach 56
Sweden 67

T
Taylor, M. 8, 16, 19
technology 112, 114-17, 123, 127-8
tele-healthcare 89
tenure
  and extra care housing 34*tab*, 39-40, 43, 101
  and financial status 28, 48-9, 52
  and retirement villages 32, 34*tab*, 47, 50-1, 53-4
  see also home ownership; mixed tenure
'tenure blind' approach 6, 103
territoriality and place attachment 89

Thinking Village project, York 106
'third age' 1, 2
'third way' approach 1, 47
Thomas, D.N. 14
Tia Hua Court, Middlesbrough 99
Tinker, A. 44
toilets in local community 112, 113
tolerance and diversity 93, 98
Tönnies, F. 8, 74
Touchmark village, Alberta 65
traffic and social interaction 17, 80, 111
transport issues 84, 110, 112, 113
Tuckett, A. 110

U
United States 67, 89, 116
  retirement villages 59-65, 68, 93, 120-1
university-based retirement communities (UBRCs) in US 65
urban redevelopment sites 44, 45, 54, 55, 118
Urban Task Force 17, 53-4, 94
US Administration on Ageing 63
Uzzell, D. 101

V
Vallelly, S.
  extra care housing and dementia 47, 97, 98, 135-6
  and social activities provision 82
  social wellbeing and extra care housing study (with Evans) 3, 4, 74, 75, 76, 77, 81, 82, 84, 87-8, 96, 98, 103, 138-40
very sheltered housing 35
  see also extra care housing
Victoria Gardens, Florida 65
villages
  local communities and loss of services 110
  and location of retirement villages 84-6
  use of term 71-2
Villages, The, Florida 60-1, 62-3

W
Ward-Thompson, C. 79
Warr, P. 82
Watts, B. 8, 24
Weiss, R.S. 9
wellbeing *see* health and wellbeing; social wellbeing
Wellman, B. 116
Wenger, C.G. 9
Westbury Fields, Bristol 3-4, 53, 55, 95-6, 98, 136-8
Whiteley village 32, 55
Willmott, P. 9
Windle, G. 117
Woolever, C. 12
World Health Organization (WHO): Age-Friendly Cities initiative 24, 83, 112, 126

Y
young people
  fear of 25, 106, 128
  see also intergenerational contact